ASPECTS

About the Author

Robin Antepara is an astrologer, writer, and educator who divides her time between Japan and Vermont. She is working on a Ph.D. in depth psychology and has master's degrees in education and psychology. Antepara is a member of the International Society for Astrological Research and has been conducting astrological seminars and workshops in Japan and North America for over ten years.

SPECIAL TOPICS IN ASTROLOGY

ASPECTS

A New Approach to Understanding
the Planetary Relationships in
Your Chart

ROBIN ANTEPARA

Llewellyn Publications
Woodbury, Minnesota

First Edition
First Printing, 2006

Series design and format by Donna Burch
Edited by Andrea Neff
Cover art © PhotoDisc and DigitalStock
Cover design by Ellen Dahl
Llewellyn is a registered trademark of Llewellyn Worldwide, Ltd.

Chart wheels were produced by the Kepler program by permission of Cosmic Patterns Software, Inc. (www.AstroSoftware.com)

Library of Congress Cataloging-in-Publication Data (Pending)
ISBN-13: 978-0-7387-0928-4
ISBN-10: 0-7387-0928-X

Llewellyn Publications
A Division of Llewellyn Worldwide, Ltd.
2143 Wooddale Drive, Dept. 0-7387-0928-X
Woodbury, MN 55125-2989, U.S.A.
www.llewellyn.com

Printed in the United States of America

Other Books in Llewellyn's Special Topics in Astrology Series

Chiron, by Martin Lass
(2005)

Vocations, by Noel Tyl
(2005)

Eclipses, by Celeste Teal
(2006)

Houses, by Gwyneth Bryan
(2006)

Venus, by Anne Massey
(2006)

Contents

List of Charts . . . xi
Introduction: Why Aspects Matter . . . 1

Part One—Working with Hard Aspects

CHAPTER ONE—THE OPPOSITION . . . 15
The Fixed Opposition: Mahatma Gandhi and the Birth of Passive Resistance . . . 17
The Mutable Opposition: Lance Armstrong, Cancer, and the Paradox of Enlightenment . . . 20
The Cardinal Opposition: Eric Harris and the Rage of the Underdog . . . 24

CHAPTER TWO—THE SQUARE . . . 29
The Fixed Square: Princess Diana . . . 31
The Mutable (and Cardinal) Square: Princess Masako of Japan . . . 34

CHAPTER THREE—THE CONJUNCTION . . . 41
The Cardinal Conjunction: Katharine Graham . . . 43
The Mutable Conjunction: Charles Schulz . . . 47
The Fixed Conjunction: Martha Stewart . . . 49

Part Two—Working with Soft Aspects

CHAPTER FOUR—THE TRINE . . . 57
The Fire Trine: Martha Stewart . . . 57
The Air Trine: Rush Limbaugh and Jane Fonda . . . 61
The Water Trine: Kurt Cobain . . . 64
The Earth Trine: Katharine Hepburn . . . 67

CHAPTER FIVE—THE SEXTILE . . . 71

John Nash . . . 73

CHAPTER SIX—THE FIRE GRAND TRINE . . . 79

Marlon Brando . . . 79

CHAPTER SEVEN—THE EARTH GRAND TRINE . . . 87

Muhammad Ali . . . 87

CHAPTER EIGHT—THE AIR GRAND TRINE . . . 95

Lance Armstrong . . . 95

The United States of America . . . 99

CHAPTER NINE—THE WATER GRAND TRINE . . . 105

Kurt Cobain . . . 105

Part Three—Other Aspects

CHAPTER TEN—THE INCONJUNCT AND THE YOD . . . 113

The Inconjunct . . . 113

The Yod . . . 115

Henry Miller . . . 116

Marlon Brando . . . 120

Martha Stewart . . . 122

CHAPTER ELEVEN—NON-PTOLEMAIC ASPECTS . . . 125

The Semisquare . . . 125

The Sesquiquadrate . . . 135

The Quintile . . . 142

The Quindecile . . . 146

CHAPTER TWELVE—TECHNIQUES OF TRANSFORMATION . . . 151

Defense Mechanisms of the Psyche . . . 152

Techniques of Transformation: Trining Your Squares and Squaring Your Trines . . . 153

Trining Your Squares: Strategies for Dealing with Hard Aspects . . . 153

Steam Control: Utilizing the Easy Places in Your Chart to Alchemize
    the Hard Places . . . 158

Squaring Your Trines: Techniques for Working with Soft Aspects . . . 162

End Word . . . 167

Appendix I: A Primer of Basic Astrology . . . 169

  The Planets . . . 169

  The Signs . . . 170

  Rulerships—Dignities—Debilities . . . 171

  Aspects . . . 172

  The Houses . . . 173

Appendix II: Chart Sources . . . 175

Bibliography . . . 177

Charts

1. The Signs . . . 4

2. Maiko . . . 7

3. The Signs, Elements, and Modalities . . . 10

4. The Opposition—180° . . . 16

5. Mahatma Gandhi . . . 18

6. Lance Armstrong . . . 22

7. Eric Harris . . . 26

8. The Square—90° . . . 30

9. Princess Diana . . . 31

10. Princess Masako . . . 36

11. The Conjunction—0° . . . 42

12. Katharine Graham . . . 44

13. Charles Schulz . . . 48

14. Martha Stewart . . . 50

15. The Trine—120° . . . 58

16. Martha Stewart . . . 60

17. Rush Limbaugh . . . 62

18. Jane Fonda . . . 64

19. Kurt Cobain . . . 66

20. Katharine Hepburn . . . 68

21. The Sextile—60° . . . 72

22. John Nash . . . 74

23. The Fire Grand Trine . . . 80

24. Marlon Brando . . . 82

25. The Earth Grand Trine . . . 88

26. Muhammad Ali . . . 90

27. The Air Grand Trine . . . 96

28. Lance Armstrong . . . 97

29. USA, Gemini Ascendant . . . 101

30. The Water Grand Trine . . . 106

31. Kurt Cobain . . . 108

32. The Inconjunct—150° . . . 114

33. The Yod . . . 115

34. Henry Miller . . . 117

35. Marlon Brando . . . 121

36. Martha Stewart . . . 123

37. The Semisquare—45° . . . 126

38. Princess Diana . . . 127

39. Marlon Brando . . . 128

40. Martha Stewart . . . 130

41. Princess Masako . . . 132

42. The Sesquiquadrate—135° . . . 134

43. Martha Stewart . . . 136

44. Princess Diana . . . 138

45. Thomas Merton . . . 140

46. The Quintile—72° . . . 142

47. Lance Armstrong . . . 143

48. Eric Harris . . . 145

49. The Quindecile—165° . . . 146

50. Eric Harris . . . 147

51. Marlon Brando . . . 149

52. Bill Clinton . . . 164

53. Synastry Biwheel for Bill and Hillary Clinton . . . 165

Why Aspects Matter

"That Doesn't Make Sense!"

Several months ago I was giving an astrology workshop in which participants were exploring the four elements—fire, air, earth, and water—and their influence in the natal chart. At one point, Maiko, a Japanese woman from Tokyo, raised her hand. "I don't understand it," she said. "I have five planets in earth, including Sun in Capricorn. Earth is very practical and business-minded, right? But I'm so imaginative!"

I walked across the room and glanced at her chart, and lo and behold, she had a strong aspect between Mars and Neptune. Neptune is the god of the sea and is associated with the imagination, creativity, and mysticism. I told her this. "And by the way," I said, "Walt Disney was another person with four planets in earth and an aspect between Neptune and Mars. So there is a suggestion here that you could put your creative energies to use in a very concrete way, perhaps some day running your own business."

Her eyes lit up. A big Disney fan, Maiko could immediately relate. Suddenly she understood something about astrology—and herself—that she had not known before.

Aspects are relationships and energetic exchanges between planets that can influence a person's chart in profound ways. Aspects are the gateway to a deeper understanding of your natal chart. When simplistic Sun sign astrology doesn't make sense—as in the case of

Maiko's chart—aspects help create a more comprehensible picture. And even when you've worked out the sign placements of the rest of the planets—Moon in Taurus, or Mars in Sagittarius, etc.—any aspects to these planets (or the lack thereof) will tell you how best to utilize those energies. Aspects are a way of unlocking potential and utilizing all your talents.

Like all relationships, aspects can be harmonious or challenging. In this book we'll consider both types and how to work with them creatively. And we'll take on a sacred cow of old school astrology: that challenging aspects are "bad" and flowing, harmonious aspects are "good." In fact, an argument could be made for the reverse: it's the challenging aspects that are ultimately best. Harmonious aspects, while not bad, are not all they're cracked up to be.

But more on that later. For now we'll examine what it is that makes an aspect harmonious or challenging (or "soft" or "hard," as we'll mostly refer to them). To do that, we need to understand the four elements and how they harmonize or blend in a birth chart.

The Elements

Imagine, for a moment, that a natal chart is like a convention: there are ten delegates (the planets), each with their own agenda, each jockeying for power and influence. There's warlike Mars, sparring for a fight; peaceable Venus, trying to mediate; and rational Mercury, attempting to put the whole thing into some sort of rational perspective.

Each of the delegates belongs to a faction (the four elements), an affiliation that changes according to one's birth date, time, and place. Thus we speak of the Sun being in earth or Mercury in air. (We'll later see how this translates into Sun in Capricorn, Mercury in Gemini, etc.) The element of a planet colors its character and also affects its ability to act. For example, the Moon in Cancer (water) is strong, while the Moon in Leo or Sagittarius (fire) is far less so.

The four elements are very important. They provide the energetic foundation for the twelve signs and are the raw materials of both psyche and cosmos. The elements are the building blocks of consciousness, the very stuff out of which our waking thoughts and impulses arise. People with no knowledge of astrology speak of colleagues and friends as "earthy" or "fiery." Nine times out of ten, those apparently non-astrological descriptions have precise correlations to one's natal chart.

The Elements as Personality Types

As we can see, the elements have profound psychological implications. It's not surprising that they correspond to two universally recognized personality types:

- Yin/Introverted: earth and water
- Yang/Extroverted: fire and air

Yin is yielding and receptive. While considered "feminine," it refers not only to women but to the feminine in all of us, what Jung called *anima*. It is our ability to listen and receive. Most importantly, it indicates the urge to bond with others and find identity in that bonding. This is represented astrologically by water (emotional bonding) and earth (physical bonding, procreation).

Yang is active and outgoing. Called *animus* by Jung, it is the need to develop ourselves as autonomous individuals and promote our interests in the world. Fire indicates the energy for the ambitious act of individuation, and air the discernment needed for that endeavor.

Many psychologists and sociologists have written of the importance of developing both sides of our psyches. Because both are so crucial for human evolution, we would ideally have a balance between the two. If we are too yin, we run the risk of codependency, or what psychoanalyst R. D. Laing called engulfment: losing our boundaries and dissolving into the other. If, on the other hand, we're too yang, we run the risk of hubris and inflation. One of the goals of this book is to explore the tension between these two deep needs. Aspects can help us determine to what extent we're imbalanced by seeing where conflicts lie. They also give us hints and suggestions as to how to realign ourselves and achieve a better balance.

We can break down the elements further in terms of Jung's four psychological types:

- Energy:[1] fire (Aries, Sagittarius, Leo)
- Thinking: air (Gemini, Libra, Aquarius)
- Sensing: earth (Taurus, Virgo, Capricorn)
- Feeling: water (Cancer, Scorpio, Pisces)

Fire signs are positive and enthusiastic. They see the glass as half full and are passionately engaged in their environments. They rebound quickly from upset and are always ready for

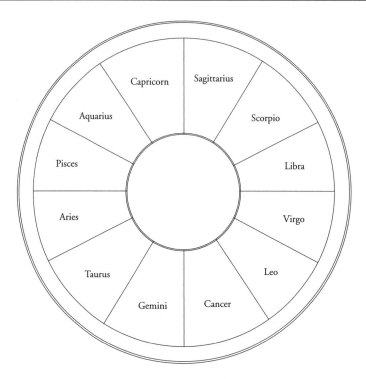

Chart 1: The Signs

a challenge. "Challenge," in fact, is their life blood, the thing that keeps them going. They possess a passion and enthusiasm that are infectious (though sometimes overbearing).

The fire archetypes are:

- Aries: the Warrior

- Leo: the Life Giver

- Sagittarius: the Explorer

Like fire, air signs are extroverted, but much more cerebral. Unlike fire, air signs are able to take a few steps back from whatever situation they're in and view it with detachment. They like to mull over their experiences and then talk and write about them with anyone who will listen. Communication and relationships are keywords for all the air signs.

The air archetypes are:

- Gemini: the Communicator/Networker

- Libra: the Mediator/Peacemaker

- Aquarius: the Reformer

Water signs, the first of the two yin elements, are emotional and empathetic—the psychics of the zodiac. As soon as they walk into a room, they hone in on people's feelings, sometimes experiencing them as their own. They make natural counselors and caregivers. They relate via the heart, not the head.

The water archetypes are:

- Cancer: the Homemaker

- Scorpio: the Transformer

- Pisces: the Healer

Earth signs are also empathetic, but in a more sensual way. They are profoundly connected to the physical world, whether this be the body, a vegetable garden, or the nickels and dimes in a cash register. Capricorns, in particular, are known for their prowess in business, while Virgos are more associated with the healing professions, and Taurus with farming. All three react viscerally to their environment.

The three earth archetypes are:

- Taurus: the Farmer

- Virgo: the Healer

- Capricorn: the Manager

Aspects: Challenging or Harmonious?

We're now ready to address the question of what makes an aspect challenging or harmonious. It's easy to see that fire and air go together—air fans and enlarges fire. Earth and water also naturally harmonize, with water being essential for a garden to grow and flourish.

On the other hand, fire and water are distinctly incompatible, as are fire and earth, or water and air. Fire scorches earth, and water douses fire, while typhoon winds destroy crops.

As a *general* rule (there are exceptions in the form of oppositions and conjunctions, which we'll consider shortly), when planets are in compatible elements, they get along;

when placed in incompatible elements, they clash. From these principles arise hard and soft aspects.

Hard Aspects: Squares, Oppositions, and Conjunctions

- Planets in fire contacting planets in water form 90° aspects called *squares* (□).
- Planets in fire contacting planets in air form 180° aspects called *oppositions* (☍).
- Planets within 7° of each other, either within or across sign lines, are called *conjunctions* (☌).

Although conjunctions mostly occur within the same sign/element, they are considered challenging by most astrologers. Imagine the strain you would feel if shackled to someone, hand and foot, for the rest of your life. This would be difficult in the best of circumstances, let alone if you and your "partner" were radically different. This is the predicament of planets in conjunction: they're very powerful—perhaps the *most* powerful of all the aspects—but extremely intense.

Similarly,

- Planets in earth contacting planets in fire form squares.
- Planets in earth contacting planets in water form oppositions.

Hard aspects foster feelings of conflict and disquietude. They create tension that must be resolved. With hard aspects, two incompatible "voices" in the psyche come into contact; the native, through conscious effort, must make adjustments in order for both to function productively. There's a host of psychological problems and challenges that can arise as a result of hard aspects (including projection, splitting, and codependency), which we'll examine at length in later chapters.

Returning to Maiko's chart, we see Neptune in Sagittarius squaring Mars in Virgo. Because Mars rules the chart (Aries Ascendant), it is especially important.

Soft Aspects: Sextiles and Trines

- Planets in fire contacting planets in air form 60° aspects called *sextiles* (✱).
- Planets in fire contacting planets in fire form 120° aspects called *trines* (△).

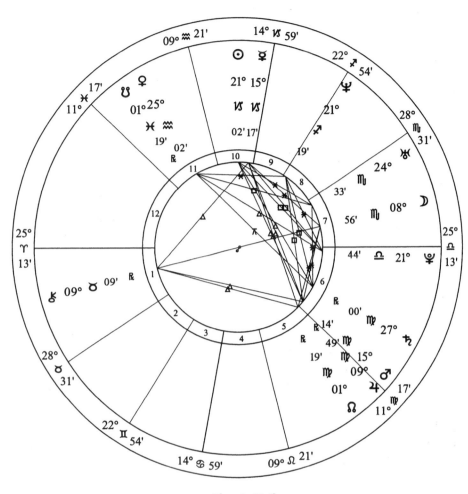

Chart 2: Maiko
January 12, 1980 / 11:23 a.m. JST
Tokyo, Japan / Placidus houses

Likewise,

- Planets in earth contacting planets in water form sextiles.
- Planets in earth contacting other planets in earth form trines.

These soft, flowing contacts endow the native with a feeling of comfort, of being in tune and at ease. For example, Uranus square the Sun (say, in fire and earth) sets up a conflict between tradition and innovation, whereas Uranus trine the Sun enables the native to spontaneously express the Uranian ideals of innovation and originality through his or her Sun sign.

Modalities/Quadruplicities

What is the difference between a sextile (fire to air, or earth to water) and an opposition (same combinations)? Both link compatible elements, and yet one is hard and the other is soft. How could the same elemental exchange be challenging in one instance and harmonious in the next? The reason is the modalities, which we will now explore.

Just as every delegate at our convention has an elemental affiliation, so too will she or he belong to a modality. There are three:

- Cardinal: Aries, Cancer, Libra, Capricorn
- Fixed: Taurus, Leo, Scorpio, Aquarius
- Mutable: Gemini, Virgo, Sagittarius, Pisces

Thus, each sign has *both* an element and a modality.

The cardinal signs are the self-starters of the universe. They initiate things, whether conversation topics, business ventures, or relationships. It's no mistake that Capricorn is most often associated with managerial ability, because when you combine earth with the self-starting impetus of the cardinal mode, you find people who operate with marked effectiveness in the business world.

This initiating energy is modified for each of the other three elements—it's emotionally based in Cancer, more cerebral in Libra, and raw and impulsive in Aries. Regardless of element, if you're ever in need of a cardinal sign, listen in on a conversation and see who initiates topics—chances are they'll have a cardinal Sun (and/or Moon).

The fixed signs are fixed: stubborn, with well-defined (and extremely hard to change) notions of who they are and what they want in life. This is one reason that Taurus (fixed earth) is known for being one of the most stubborn signs of the zodiac. Earth in and of itself is "fixed" and unchanging. Add to that the fixity of the modal vibration, and you get one heck of a stubborn sign. Aquarius, Leo, and Scorpio are stubborn as well, but with more innate flexibility than the dependable Taurus.

The mutable signs are the ones that go with the flow. Their boundaries are much more permeable than either the cardinal or fixed signs. Who they are is always changing and open to redefinition. This is the least true for Virgo (mutable earth) and the most true for Pisces (mutable water) and Gemini (mutable air). This is one reason that Pisces is so often associated with mysticism, creativity, and—on the shadow side—addiction and insanity. When the ego boundaries are as permeable (and emotional) as mutable water would suggest, one must be especially careful to maintain a solid sense of self.

We can now understand why sextiles are flowing and oppositions challenging. Both combine compatible elements, but sextiles link *two different modalities* while oppositions link two of the same. With different modalities, there is more give and take, more room for maneuvering and negotiation. Throwing two modal signs together, whether in an opposition or square, is too close. "Familiarity breeds contempt" is the watch phrase here.

Trining Your Squares and Squaring Your Trines: The Astrology of Transformation

This book presents cases of how famous people worked creatively with both hard and soft aspects. Although many think the main challenge of a natal chart lies in alchemizing one's hard aspects, we'll see that soft aspects are every bit as challenging, although for different reasons. To successfully manage the energies in your chart, you must learn not only to trine your squares but to square your trines.

Trining Your Squares

Hard aspects are challenging because they link either incompatible elements or similar elements in stressful combinations. Translated into psychological terms, hard aspects often indicate our shadow sides—unconscious facets of self. One hundred years of psychological research has taught us that the psyche is like an iceberg: the tip is consciousness, and the vast, unseen region below is the unconscious. By necessity, most of that subterranean region must remain in shadow—lest we become engulfed by its contents and consumed by psychosis. But if *all* of it is hidden all the time, big problems arise. "The psychological rule," wrote Carl Jung, "says that when an inner situation is not made conscious, it happens outside, as fate. That is to say, when the individual remains undivided and does not become conscious of his inner opposite, the world must perforce act out the conflict and be torn into opposing halves."[2] Ultimately, we must take responsibility for *all* of who we are, whether we're conscious of it or not.

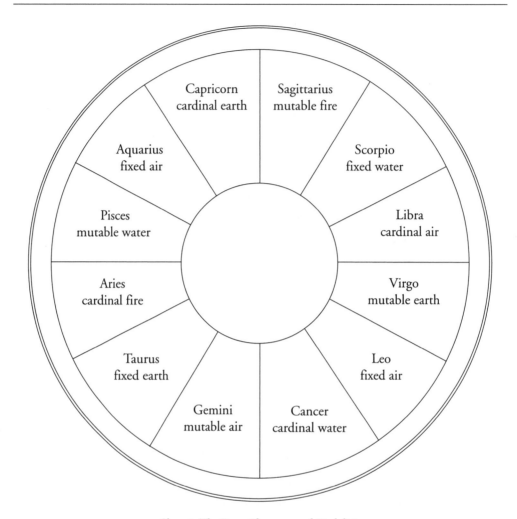

Chart 3: The Signs, Elements, and Modalities

One's astrology chart—and particularly the hard aspects—is a powerful diagnostic tool for shining light on areas of unconsciousness. We look to squares, oppositions, and conjunctions (and later, inconjuncts and semisquares) to obtain valuable information about our blind spots and, in so doing, recognize self-defeating behavior patterns.

The case histories presented in this book will help you identify practical ways of trining your squares and living a more productive life. For example, if you have Sun in Aries square Moon in Cancer, you're faced with the challenge of making a fire planet work with a water planet. How can this be done? The two don't go together. However, if you do something creative—like put the water in a pot and the pot on a stove—there are *loads* of opportunities available, many more than if you had Sun in Aries trine Moon in Sagittarius. Not that the latter is bad. But without the tension brought on by the water-fire combo, it's unlikely you'll be motivated to do something creative with that pairing. Complacency and inaction are much more likely with the soft aspects.

Squaring Your Trines

Unless, that is, you're aware of astrology and able to work consciously with the *ease* of that contact and do something different with it. Thus, the challenge with soft aspects (whether trines or sextiles) is to recognize your inclination to be complacent in that area and *consciously* choose the road less traveled. "Your enemy is your best teacher," say the Tibetan Buddhists. With squares, oppositions, and conjunctions, this enemy is forced upon us. With soft aspects, we have to act as our own "enemy": we have to become the stick-wielding Zen master. In so doing, we not only learn about shadow aspects of ourselves but unlock potential we never knew we had.

A Note on the Organization of This Book

This book is divided into parts—Part One: Working with Hard Aspects and Part Two: Working with Soft Aspects. Each chapter examines a Ptolemaic aspect vis-à-vis profiles of famous people, each one focusing on a different modality.

Each chapter also examines the relative importance of the aspect to the life of the native. In astrology, specific planets, signs, houses, etc., have no real meaning in and of themselves but only in relation to the whole. For each person, then, we examine the relative importance and weight it has in the context of the total chart. For example, Gandhi's opposition in Taurus/Scorpio played a major role in his life. Lance Armstrong's Jupiter-Saturn opposition was less important, although it did play a crucial role when he was diagnosed with cancer.

---

1. Jung postulated "intuition" as the fourth type; here, however, we will substitute "energy," as it is closer to describing the essence of fire.

2. Carl Jung, *Psyche and Symbol* (Princeton, NJ: Princeton University Press, 1991), p. 70.

PART ONE

Working with Hard Aspects

CHAPTER ONE

The Opposition

- 180° hard aspect
- Keywords: polarity, awareness

The opposition is like a dual at dawn: two (or more) planets standing face to face, eyeing each other with laser intensity. While widely acknowledged to be a challenging aspect, the opposition doesn't present conflicting energies, as in a square, but complementary energies with razor-sharp awareness. Thus we find aggression and mediation (Aries/Libra), sensuality and sexuality (Taurus/Scorpio), and nurture and control (Cancer/Capricorn), to name just three.

There are two ways in which the opposition manifests. In the first, there's a super-amplification of the energies, as if the planets on both sides were shining spotlights on each other. Because this generates so much momentum, it has a tendency to throw the chart as a whole off balance. If the planets in the opposition are particularly strong (i.e., if they're exalted or dignified), the potential for imbalance is all the greater. (See the section "Rulerships—Dignities—Debilities" in appendix I.)

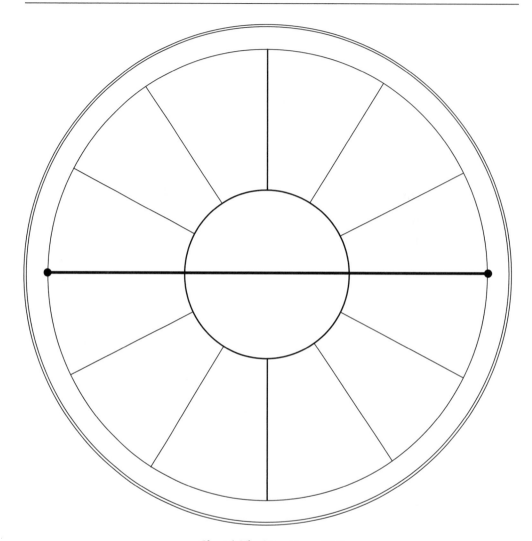

Chart 4: The Opposition—180°

The second way the opposition can manifest is in a seesawing back-and-forth between the two sides, with one or the other dominant. The challenge is to find a middle way between the two and integrate *both* into one's personality.

The following are case studies examining how three people dealt with their oppositions. We'll see how both Gandhi and Lance Armstrong were able to work productively with theirs, while Eric Harris got tangled up in the shadow side of the planetary energies and perished.

The Fixed Opposition:
Mahatma Gandhi and the Birth of Passive Resistance

Mahatma Gandhi was one of the greatest leaders the world has ever seen. He was born on October 2, 1869, at a time when India was under British rule (chart 5). When Gandhi first embarked on his career as a lawyer, he was so shy he could hardly speak. He tells of one incident at a provincial courthouse where he was representing his first client. He had meticulously prepared for the case, but when he got up to speak, he was tongue-tied. "My heart sank into my boots," he said. "My head was reeling and I felt as though the whole court was doing likewise. I could think of no question to ask." Gandhi sat down without having uttered a word, handing over the case to a colleague for whom the case was "child's play."[1]

Was this really the same man who led massive political rallies and toppled an empire? The story of how Gandhi managed this incredible transformation from bumbler to world-renowned leader is largely the story of how he grappled with an intense opposition between Taurus and Scorpio.

War and Peace:
Venus and Mars in Scorpio Opposing Jupiter and Pluto in Taurus

Tolstoy's famous 1869 novel comes to mind here, for in Gandhi's opposition we see a microcosm of both human impulses. The gods of war are well represented, with Mars symbolizing the urge for worldly power, and both Pluto and Scorpio the marshaling of those inner resources needed to ensure survival. All three are associated with raw, instinctual impulses, including the lust for revenge.

In the midst of this mayhem is Taurus and her ruler, Venus. Venus signifies the urge for peace and harmony; she is the mediator who wants to keep everyone happy. However, as we saw in the introduction, there is another, deeper urge: our desire to be deeply connected with our fellow beings. Conversely, Mars symbolizes not only war but the desire for

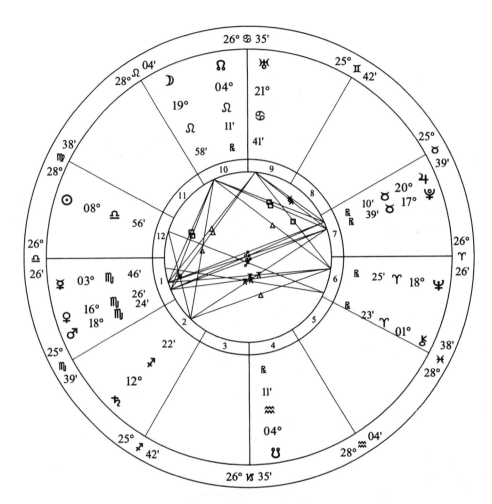

Chart 5: Mahatma Gandhi
October 2, 1869 / 7:11 a.m. LMT
Porbandar, India / Placidus houses

individuation and self-development. Whenever the Mars and Venus archetypes are brought into contact, the essential challenge is not only to resolve tensions between aggression and conciliation but to forge a balance between the need for intimacy and autonomy.

There are several other factors that make this configuration especially powerful. Gandhi's opposition is composed of two intense conjunctions (Venus-Mars and Jupiter-Pluto), and it's part of a t-square involving the Moon. (Both will be explored in later chapters.) In addition, there is a mutual reception involving Venus in Scorpio (Pluto's sign) and Pluto in Taurus (Venus's sign). In mutual receptions, both fields become electrically charged, transforming the two planets into a dynamic duo. For Gandhi, that meant being able to express Venusian ideals with Plutonic intensity, and Plutonic power with Venusian overtones. We'll see how this helped set the stage for the birth of passive resistance.

The Role of the Opposition in Gandhi's Chart

This opposition played a pivotal role in Gandhi's chart, thanks to Venus's rulership of both his Libra Sun and Ascendant. As a result, the energies of the opposition were hard-wired into Gandhi's psyche. Because this opposition played out in the first and seventh houses, these energies were immediately apparent to all who came in contact with him. Many have described the charisma and the steely will he exuded (Pluto-Scorpio), while others remarked on his gentle and peaceable presence. Both were part of who he was.

The Astrology of Transformation: The Birth of Passive Resistance

How did Gandhi reconcile the tension of his opposition? In the beginning of his life it was as if he had split off the Mars-Pluto energies from consciousness, refusing to own or even acknowledge his immense power (thus his paralyzing shyness in the courtroom). In so doing, he (unconsciously) assigned himself to play the hapless victim.

However, in other ways he was very much in touch with his animal impulses. He wrote of his "lustful cruelty" in the early years of his marriage, and of how he bullied his illiterate wife.[2] A kind of "victim-perpetrator" continuum developed in his psyche as a result, with Gandhi veering back and forth between the two extremes.

Slowly, he began to integrate both side of the opposition into awareness. He did this in two ways: through controlling/alchemizing the passion of the Mars-Pluto-Scorpio placements and through the path of service.

Self-control played a major role in his life. Gandhi was a strict vegetarian. This practice started in childhood with his family's vegetarian lifestyle. By the time of his death, Gandhi was eating only fruits and nuts. The need for self-control also manifested in his decision, at age thirty-six, to become celibate. "So overpowering are the senses that they can be kept under control only when they are completely hedged in on all sides," he wrote.[3]

The ultimate expression of Gandhi's self-control manifested in his embrace of passive resistance and in his astounding ability *not* to strike back when accosted. Here we see the mutual reception mentioned earlier—Venusian ideals of peace enacted with Scorpionic intensity. Anyone who has seen dramatizations of Gandhi being bludgeoned and bloodied and not raising a finger to fight back understands the power of the Venus-Pluto mutual reception in his chart.

In the resolution of his opposition, Gandhi redefined what it meant to wield power. In the beginning of his life, the British were omnipotent: they called the shots and Indians obeyed. The Indian people could hardly do otherwise given the amount of military hardware arrayed against them. Gandhi's achievement lay in transforming "powerlessness"—the lack of guns and technology, the refusal to fight back—into an expression of profound strength. In the merging and melding of the Venus, Pluto, and Mars energies, he had discovered a greater power called love, one he called "the subtlest force in the world."[4] This brings to mind the words of another great pacifist, Pierre Teilhard de Chardin, who described this great force in a similar way: "Someday, after mastering the winds, the waves, the tides and gravity, we shall harness for God the energies of love, and then, for the second time in the history of the world, man will have discovered fire."[5]

This leads us to the second means through which Gandhi alchemized the polarities of his opposition: the path of service. It was not for himself but for the sake of Indian migrant workers that he was able to withstand repeated blows from the police in South Africa. It was not for his own good but for the good of the Indian people that he defied British occupation forces in India, spending months at a time locked up behind bars. These two things—self-restraint and service—are intertwined, of course: through self-restraint one becomes aware of the needs and aches of the Other, and through service one develops love and compassion.

The Mutable Opposition:
Lance Armstrong, Cancer, and the Paradox of Enlightenment

Lance Armstrong came from an unlikely background for a champion. The seven-time winner of the Tour de France was born to a seventeen-year-old single mother who struggled to make ends meet. He grew up in a town known as the heroin capital of the country and had to scratch and claw for every small success, from being accepted at a conformist high school to duking it out with an abusive stepfather who appeared on the scene when he was three.

Into this apparently dead-end scenario came one ray of hope: a bicycle. For the raging adolescent who felt fenced in at both home and school, this was a dream come true. The bike, Lance said, was "liberation and independence," his first set of wheels.[6]

It wasn't long before Armstrong was placing in regional competitions. At age sixteen he was named National Rookie of the Year, and by the time he was twenty-five he was on the verge of breaking into the top five in international rankings. Through it all, he developed what can only be described as a super-macho persona: mouthing off at opponents, getting into scrapes with motorists, and ignoring his coach's advice. It was an approach to life that eschewed thinking and reason for raw impulse—one that was particularly problematic on the racetrack. Armstrong knew he had to conserve energy in the longer races in order to win, but he couldn't restrain himself—very strange behavior for someone with four planets in Virgo! (We will examine the contradiction between Lance's macho persona and the humility suggested by this Virgo emphasis at greater length in chapter 8.)

Just when Lance felt like he was on the top of the world came a shocking development: news that he had advanced testicular cancer, which had spread to his brain and lungs. His chances of surviving were slim.

However, not only did Lance survive, but the cancer proved to be a turning point in his life, transforming him from a successful winner of one-day bike races to one of the greatest cyclists the world has seen. The engine of transformation was a spiritual awakening in which much more changed than mere racing status. The story of this transformation can be seen through the lens of his mutable opposition (chart 6).

Jupiter and Neptune in Sagittarius Opposing Saturn in Gemini

Lance's opposition links Saturn in Gemini with Jupiter-Neptune in Sagittarius. Like Gandhi, it involves a close conjunction (here between Neptune and Jupiter). Also like Gandhi, it links polar opposites: Saturn, the lord of constriction and discipline, and Jupiter, symbol of expansion, hope, and optimism. Jupiter is in its own sign, making it especially potent. Neptune suffuses this configuration with the possibility of transcendence.

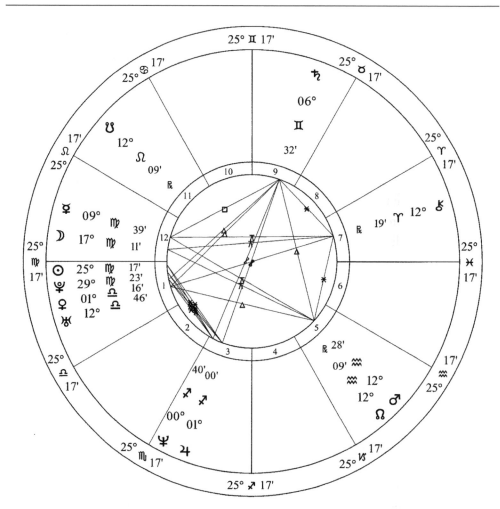

Chart 6: Lance Armstrong
September 18, 1971
Plano, Texas / Sunrise chart

Lance's powerful Jupiter comes as no surprise: Jupiter in Sagittarius is a perfect symbol for the freedom and liberation Lance feels on his bike. Indeed, the bike was a passport to a larger, better world. Saturn represents the hard work and discipline needed to channel all that mutable Jupiterian energy into champion material.

The opposition in Lance's chart is important, although not as central as Gandhi's. Unlike Gandhi, there are no planets in the opposition that are directly connected to the Sun, and the opposition is not angular.[7] However, this aspect mirrors the main challenge of his chart—the conflict between freedom and discipline. The mutable fire and air also echo a mutable Virgo stellium involving the Sun, Moon, Mercury, and Pluto. Most importantly for our purposes here, the energies of this opposition played a crucial role at a pivotal time in Lance's life: his diagnosis and recovery from cancer.

The Astrology of Transformation:
The Paradox of Enlightenment—Bigger or Smaller?

On the day Lance was diagnosed with cancer, transiting Pluto was exactly conjunct Lance's natal Jupiter, and in the months before had been seesawing back and forth over his Jupiter-Neptune conjunction. Clearly, the onset of cancer had a lot to do with Lance's strong Jupiterian urge for freedom. One could even say the cancer was a direct challenge to Lance's freewheeling ways.

Thus began a long, slow process in which the cyclist started paring himself down. Gone were the five-hour practice rides, the parties, and the photo ops. Suddenly, he found himself flat on his back in a hospital room, an intravenous drip at his side and a cocktail of deadly chemicals flowing into his bloodstream.

Through the discipline and grit endowed by Saturn, Lance was able to fight his illness. He conducted extensive research on various cancer treatments and doctors and hospitals. Lance himself concedes that, had it not been for the patience and discipline he learned during his battle with cancer, he never could have won the 2,000-mile Tour de France.

On one level, Lance was restricted and curtailed as a result of his encounter with cancer. In truly Saturnine fashion, he got smaller. However, on another level he got bigger. Thanks to the faith, hope, and love of Jupiter-Neptune, he grew to heroic proportions—starting his own foundation, raising millions of dollars for cancer victims, and becoming a father in the thick of it all. (And this is not to mention his seven consecutive wins at the Tour de France.)

But the power of Jupiter-Neptune goes even deeper. When, after brain surgery, the doctors informed him that all they'd found had been "necrotic" or dead tissue, everyone wondered why. They'd been expecting live cancer cells likely to spread to other regions of the brain. But for Lance the answer was simple: it was faith that saved him. "I believed in belief, for its own shining sake."[8]

Before his illness, Lance had never thought about religion or spirituality—he'd always been too busy. But with the stillness brought on by the cancer, he had time to reflect. And although the odds were stacked against him, Lance chose to believe. What better description could we have of Jupiter, radiant in its own sign and suffused with the healing power of Neptune, than "believing in belief"?

The Cardinal Opposition: Eric Harris and the Rage of the Underdog

We close this chapter with a contrasting look at someone who *wasn't* able to alchemize the energies of his opposition: Columbine gunman Eric Harris.

Eric Harris was born on April 9, 1981, in Plattsburgh, New York (chart 7).[9] Harris's father was a major in the Air Force, which led to multiple moves and upheavals when Eric was a child. There is a growing literature on the psychological impact that these moves have on military children, including a fear of intimacy and feelings of alienation and dislocation. Harris himself said that every time he switched schools, he had to start over, "at the bottom of the ladder."[10] In a desperate attempt to find a niche, Harris applied to the Marines. He was rejected, just three days before the Columbine massacre, after it was learned he was taking Luvox, a psychiatric drug used to treat depression and obsessive-compulsive disorder.

Harris was a misfit at school, bullied and taunted by other classmates. Many analysts have commented on the "culture of cruelty" at Columbine, and how it influenced the violence that erupted there. Others have disavowed it as a determining factor in the boys's behavior. One thing is certain: Columbine High School did not look kindly on kids who were different. Here are the comments of one football player at the school. Ostensibly about Harris and his accomplice, Dylan Klebold, they ultimately say more about the school than the boys who terrorized it: "Columbine is a clean, good place except for those rejects. Most kids didn't want them there. They were into witchcraft. They were into voodoo dolls. Sure, we teased them. But what do you expect with kids who come to school with weird hairdos and horns on their hats? It's not just jocks; the whole school's disgusted with them. They're a bunch of homos, grabbing each other's private parts. If you want to get rid of someone, usually you tease 'em. So the whole school would call them homos, and when they did something sick, we'd tell them." It was not uncommon for other kids to throw stones at members of the "Trench Coat Mafia" as they walked by.[11]

Like Gandhi, Harris saw himself as an underdog (Gandhi vis-à-vis the British Empire, Harris the Columbine elite). On one of the videotapes he and Klebold made before the shootings, Harris said they would "kick-start" a revolution of the dispossessed—exactly what Gandhi had done, but in a radically different way.[12]

Sun, Venus, and Mars in Aries Opposing Pluto in Libra

Here we see a configuration remarkably similar to Gandhi's: both had polarities between "war" (Pluto, Mars, and Aries) and "peace" (Venus and Libra). However, unlike Gandhi (and this is an important difference), the opposition is in cardinal signs. In addition, Harris's Sun is involved in this combustible mix; there is no pacifying influence, as with Gandhi's twelfth-house Sun in Libra.

Cardinal signs are more inherently unstable than fixed signs. Their impulse is always to act and move, whereas that of fixed signs is to maintain stability and control, by standing still if necessary. When fixed signs feel distress and uncertainty, they dig in their heels and wait. Cardinal signs, on the other hand, feel compelled to do something—*anything*—to alleviate the distress. This can obviously have disastrous consequences when volatile energies are involved.

This opposition is central to the chart. As already noted, it involves not only Harris's Sun but also his ruling planet (Pluto ruling his Scorpio Ascendant). There are actually two Aries-Libra oppositions in the chart: Sun, Mars, and Venus opposing Pluto, and Mercury opposite Jupiter-Saturn. In total, four of the five personal planets are tied up in these two oppositions. The fact that Harris's Cancer Moon forms a t-square to the latter does not help matters any, as we'll see in a moment.

April 20, 1999: A Tragic Playing Out of Titanic Forces

What transpired on April 20, 1999, was pretty close to what an old-school, fatalistic astrologer would expect when you put Sun, Mars, and Pluto together in hard aspect. An extreme expression of the shadow side of Aries—anger, impulsiveness, self-centeredness—opposed

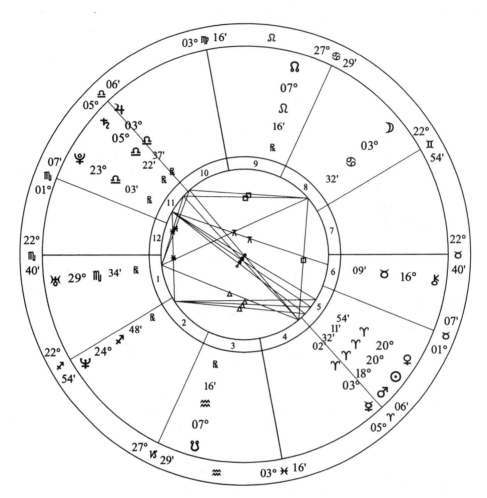

Chart 7: Eric Harris
April 9, 1981 / 9:37 p.m. CST
Wichita, Kansas / Placidus houses

the Plutonic urge to bring the hidden to light. In this case, the "hidden" involved the boys's feelings of humiliation and persecution at a conformist school. *No one* understood the depth of their angs, not even their parents: they kept it bottled up inside with Plutonic intensity. But after their grand finale, all that dark Plutonic material would be blasted, literally, to the surface. Then everyone would know.

Several factors in the chart magnify not only the explosive Aries energies but the deep sense of grievance that Harris felt. The Aries energies are particularly strong because there is a stellium (Sun, Venus, Mars, and Mercury). In addition, the Sun is exalted, and Mars is triumphant in its own sign. (See the section "Rulerships—Dignities—Debilities" in appendix I.) Dignified and exalted planets, because they are so strong, stridently insist on their rights. Here, with the Pluto opposition, they are like protesters shouting epithets at a hated authority figure.

It's also important to note that Venus in Aries is in its detriment. Planets in detriment or fall have something of a chip on their shoulders: they know they are in a weakened position and are none too happy about it. Depending on other factors in the chart (and on the planets and signs involved), that can make them quite prickly and defensive. Because Aries is involved here, the reaction is more combative than usual.

One more factor that contributes to the volatility of this opposition is Harris's Cancer Moon. Here we find another dignified planet prone to demanding its rights. Because this is a watery planet and sign, those rights are emotional, making the feelings of grievance even more acute.

Because of the presence of dignified and exalted planets, this chart is similar to the inflationary charts we will examine in Part Two: Working with Soft Aspects. As we'll see, trines and sextiles can lead to overconfidence because the flow of energy is so easy and unencumbered. There is a similar dynamic at work with dignified planets: the energies get a bit cocky because they are so strong. In Harris's chart, this created an explosive combination of overconfidence and grievance, setting up an inflationary dynamic that, once ignited, spiraled out of control.

Performance Art

There were many suggestions that Harris and Klebold saw April 20 not only as an act of vengeance but as a kind of Wagnerian grand opera, and themselves as avant-garde artists/conductors. Harris called himself "Reb," short for rebel, and Klebold signed his handiwork

"VoDKa Vengeance." Their essays at school, and the videotapes they left behind, all suggest the need to create and express (albeit in warped fashion), not only to destroy.[13]

The creative urge is reflected in Harris's chart through the accentuated fifth house. The fifth house is known for creative endeavors and self-expression of all kinds. With three personal planets there, Harris almost certainly felt a deep desire to create, and share his creations with others.

Perhaps even more than others, astrologers can see the tragedy of untapped potential in this young man's life. Had there been a thriving arts program at Columbine, or had Harris been in contact with a mentor with whom he could have channeled those artistic impulses, would the events of April 20 have taken place? We'll never know. It's clear that Harris got precious little encouragement in that direction during his short life. And yet this is precisely the kind of advice and counsel an astrologer could have offered in the months and years leading up to the massacre.

1. M. K. Gandhi, *An Autobiography* (Ahmedabad, India: Navajivan Trust, 1927), p. 79.

2. Ibid., p. 21.

3. Ibid., p. 175.

4. *M. K. Gandhi Institute for Nonviolence*, http://www.gandhiinstitute.org.

5. Pierre Teilhard de Chardin, *The Creative Process*, http://www.creativeprocess.net/gp/teilhard.html.

6. Lance Armstrong, with Sally Jenkins, *It's Not About the Bike* (New York: Berkley Books, 2000), p. 19.

7. As far as I know, Lance Armstrong's birth time is not known. The time used here was adjusted by the author. I have chosen not to discuss house placement, as that could change according to birth time.

8. Armstrong, p. 113.

9. There is a dispute about where Eric Harris was born, with some suggesting it was Wichita, Kansas, and not Plattsburgh, New York. Both locations place the Aries/Libra oppositions firmly in the fifth/eleventh houses.

10. N. Gibbs and T. Roche, "The Columbine Tapes," *Time*, December 20, 1999, p. 44.

11. Ibid.

12. Ibid.

13. Ibid.

CHAPTER TWO

The Square

- 90° hard aspect
- Incompatible elements; same modality
- Keywords: tension, conflict, challenge, projection

As we've seen, the square combines incompatible elements (fire and water, earth and fire, etc.) and the *same* modalities (cardinal with cardinal, fixed with fixed, etc.).

More than any other aspect, the square is associated with conflicting impulses and tendencies. It is also more likely than any other aspect to be projected onto someone or something in the environment. The projected qualities can be repugnant, in which case the Other is demonized; or desirable, in which case the Other is idealized. The intensity of a square can also be split off and relegated to the unconscious, where it foments trouble. One way or another, the energy will get out, if not through projections then through accidents, disease, or other unhappy circumstances of "fate."

In this chapter we examine the square as it manifests in the charts of two princesses: Diana of Britain and Masako of Japan.

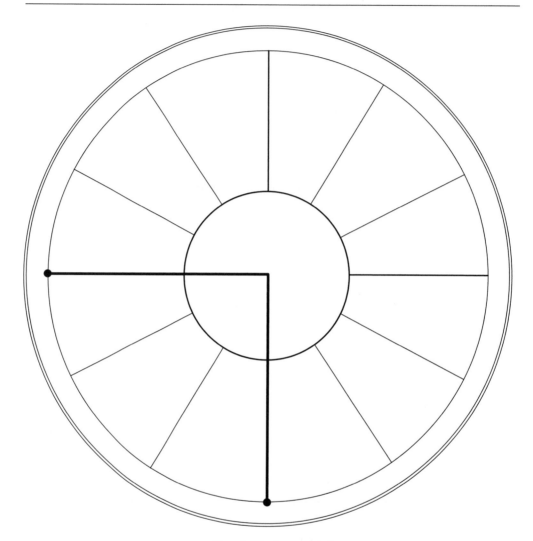

Chart 8: The Square—90°

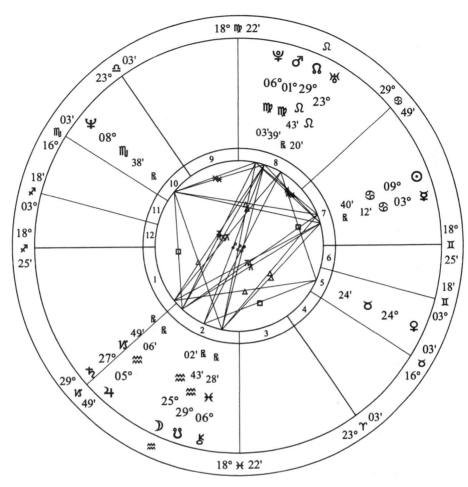

Chart 9: Princess Diana
July 1, 1961 / 7:45 p.m. GMD
Sandringham, England / Placidus houses

The Fixed Square: Princess Diana

It seems redundant to recount the facts of Diana's life, so mythic has she become. What accounts for her iconic status? Perhaps it was the union of opposites on display during her short life. Diana was the personification of power: born into an aristocratic family, she married royalty and was beautiful and glamorous to boot. Despite all this, she more often than not saw herself as a victim: although wellborn, she was an outsider in Charles's world. She had the equivalent of an eighth-grade education. To top it off, she suffered humiliation and defeat at the hands of Charles and his lover, Camilla. She exhibited deeply human vulnerabilities that repelled some and drew others inexorably into her sphere.

Indeed, vulnerability is one of the first words that comes to mind when we think of Cancer, Diana's Sun sign. A cardinal water sign ruled by the Moon, Cancer is a symbol of feminine sensitivity and compassion. Don't be fooled by the crab's hard shell—it's just there to protect the soft core. The zigzagging movements keep adversaries guessing and create an additional layer of protection.

Diana was well endowed with Cancerian vulnerability. We see this not only in the pain she suffered as a result of Charles's infidelity but in the devastation she experienced when her parents divorced. The flip side of vulnerability is compassion, something else she amply demonstrated through the affection she lavished upon her two sons.

But it was not enough for her to be a loving and devoted parent—Diana craved love and attention in return. This was something she never got from her husband. "Are you in love?" a reporter asked shortly before their wedding. "Of course!" replied the starry-eyed Diana. "Whatever love is," muttered the cerebral and detached Charles.[1]

What most people don't realize is that Diana had a similar need for detachment in intimate relationships, although it was one she never quite admitted to herself. We'll see how this need for space was expressed through a Venus-Uranus square, and later through the t-square formed with her Aquarius Moon.

Venus in Taurus Square Uranus in Leo: Princess Diana's Illusive Pursuit of Freedom

Taken alone, Venus in Taurus reinforces the Cancerian need for intimacy. A fixed earth sign, Taurus craves security and physical contact. The Cancer-Taurus combination presents two yin elements and a concomitant longing for deep human connectedness.

A very different picture forms, however, when we consider Venus's square to Uranus. Uranus is a planet associated with revolution and electricity—both of which are anathema to the Venusian need for closeness. Placed in fiery Leo, we see an urge for dramatic self-expression, another potential upset to the harmony craved by Venus.

Uranus cares not a whit for intimacy and closeness. In fact, he's downright dismayed by it. All those pesky personal needs and emotions cramp his style. Uranus sees himself as a crusader for the common good—and all the better if he can accomplish that with flair and pizzaz. When found in hard aspect to Venus, Uranus creates a need for space and detachment. This need for space can manifest in many different ways—through unions between people of vastly different ages (true for Diana and Charles) or educational levels (also true for them), as well as in international marriages where the two people come from different cultures and have radically different frames of reference. For most people, these sorts of differences would create too much space and hinder intimacy. However, for the Venus-Uranus type, it creates a kind of virtual closeness that is much more desirable than the real thing.

T-Squares and Complexes

Diana's Venus-Uranus square is part of a larger configuration known as a t-square and, for that reason, is vitally important. Venus is particularly potent because it occupies the focal position of the t-square, as well as being in her own sign. The t-square creates intense inner pressure and requires constant vigilance to prevent psychic imbalance. Astrologer Alan Oken likens it to a three-legged chair always on the verge of toppling over.[2]

Like other configurations that link three or more planets, the t-square creates a sub-system in the psyche known as a "complex": an emotionally charged nuclei of reason and emotion that functions independently of the conscious ego. Complexes may be unconscious (and repressed due to a related pain or trauma) or simply an energy that the native is unwilling and/or unable to deal with. The challenge of the t-square, as with all complexes, is to integrate the dynamic into one's personality.

The stressful linking of Venus and Uranus in Diana's chart is echoed by her Aquarius Moon. Not only does Aquarius amplify the Uranian energy, but it is the ruler of Diana's watery Cancer Sun! With this, we obtain a window into the inner psychodrama that drove this woman: Diana's very vulnerable, exquisitely sensitive Cancer Sun and—horror of horrors—the ruling Moon in the unsympathetic sign of Aquarius. Thus we see two energy systems at odds with each other: the Uranian complex of Diana's t-square (with all the attendant needs for freedom, unpredictability, and detachment) and her emotional Sun. Like an intricate Bach fugue whose voices become hopelessly entangled, the need for closeness gets pitted against an equally strong need for freedom. To top it all off, Diana's Ascendant weighs in with the freewheeling mutable fire sign of Sagittarius—another challenge to the needs of her emotional Sun.

Alchemy or Not? The Astrology of Transformation

The story of Diana's life is indeed a story of transformation, one that can be told in three acts. In act one, Diana was largely unconscious of her Uranus complex. As a result, she lived solely out of her needy Cancer Sun. The primary emphasis in her life was her work with children (one employer called her the nanny from heaven) and her close female friendships. It was as if the abundant Aquarian energies in her chart didn't exist. But this Uranus complex most definitely did exist, as she was soon to find out.

In act two, the Uranus complex was activated, albeit indirectly, through Charles and Camilla. Charles's remoteness and detachment were issues in the relationship long before Camilla was publicly acknowledged as playing a role. Diana found notes and trinkets from Camilla even before their wedding day. When Diana objected, Charles shrugged them off as being gifts from a friend. After the birth of Harry, Camilla reappeared with a vengeance, and Diana's eating disorders began. The cause? From all appearances, Charles's unfaithfulness.[3]

However, the advent of an unfaithful husband was Diana projecting outward her own unconscious need for space. She did so because this complex of energies was unacceptable; it clashed with the needs of her sensitive Cancer Sun. It would take many years for Diana to integrate these Uranian energies into her personality.

This happened in the third and final act when Diana embarked on humanitarian work, ministering to people with AIDS, battered wives, and cancer survivors, among others. People who were poor and downtrodden, the people no one else cared about—these were the people Diana embraced in her secular ministry. Here we see the deep compassion of Diana's Cancer Sun expressed in a completely different context. It was a context, mind you, that permitted her the freedom craved by her Aquarian Moon and Venus-Uranus square. She could get up from the AIDS ward and walk away at any time; not so with her marriage. This was the same reason she finally did get up and walk away: the Uranian energies, and the fixity of the Taurus-Leo square, would settle for nothing less.

The Mutable (and Cardinal) Square: Princess Masako of Japan

The daughter of a diplomat, Masako is the epitome of a Sagittarius Sun: international, fluent in four languages, sophisticated. As a result of her father's postings, she went to kindergarten in Moscow, elementary school in New York, and high school in Boston. She attended two of the most elite universities in the world—Harvard, where she received a B.A.

in economics, and the University of Tokyo. In 1987 she accepted a career-track position with the Japanese foreign ministry. She was seen as being one of a handful of women who would lead Japan into the twenty-first century.

It was around the time that Masako accepted the job with the foreign ministry that Crown Prince Naruhito started getting desperate to find a wife. Rumor had it that Masako's father, himself highly placed in the ministry, was being pressured (some same threatened) to offer up his daughter as a bride to Naruhito. Whether or not that rumor was true, Masako did agree to the match, whereupon her own promising career came to an abrupt halt.

It was hoped that because of her education and breadth of experience, Masako would help modernize the role of the Crown Princess in Japan. She is seen as being one of the most accomplished women to ever set foot in the imperial palace.[4]

Sadly, that has not been the case. Instead, she has withered away. Her main responsibility, as the imperial bureaucrats see it, is to produce an heir to the Chrysanthemum Throne, and she has been under relentless pressure to do so since her 1993 marriage. After several miscarriages, Masako did give birth to a baby girl in 2001, but there have been no children since. Some people have been calling for a change in the constitution in order to permit a woman (Masako's daughter) to ascend the throne. The Imperial Household Agency, though, has refused, saying only a son will suffice.[5]

In the winter of 2004, Masako was diagnosed with stress-induced shingles and went into seclusion. It was rumored that she was also suffering from depression and taking low-dosage medication. "Masako has essentially become a prisoner," one reporter said.[6] Meanwhile, there's been an outcry from the Japanese public against the Imperial Household Agency, with one weekly demanding that the ruling mandarins "stop stamping out Masako's personality."[7]

Sun in Sagittarius Square Uranus-Pluto in Virgo: Power versus Freedom

This square presents a very complicated picture, not only astrologically but in terms of the cultural context in which this planetary drama is being played out (chart 10).

On one side is the Sun—symbol of life force and will. On the other we find two powerhouse planets, Pluto and Uranus, yoked in a tight conjunction. Either of these planets alone would be a handful in hard aspect to the Sun. With both of them, the pressure can be overwhelming.

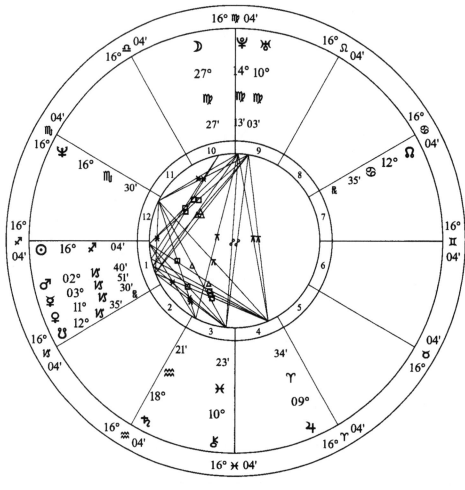

Chart 10: Princess Masako
December 9, 1963
Tokyo, Japan / Sunrise chart

Pluto and the Abduction of the Will

The effect of Pluto in hard aspect to personal planets can be compared to the abduction story in the myth of Hades and Persephone. One day while Persephone was picking flowers, she was carried off to the underworld by Hades. After a long search, her mother, Demeter, rescued her, but not before Persephone had been irrevocably altered. As in myth, so in life: when Pluto aspects personal planets, especially the Sun, there are episodes of structural change to the personality, a time when the entire psychic structure is reorganized from the bottom up.

Because this is a square, there is a greater likelihood of the Plutonic abductor being projected onto a force outside the self. In Masako's case, Pluto has manifested in the form of her Imperial minders, a cadre of officials known throughout Japan for their secrecy and conservatism. Although it was the Prince who asked for her hand in marriage, it is the palace bureaucrats who control every detail (Virgo) of Masako's life. Unlike jet-setting royalty in other countries, Masako and her husband rarely set foot outside the palace—there are no discreet dinners out at expensive restaurants. Even her telephone calls must be routed through (and approved by) imperial officials. For someone brought up in a cosmopolitan, multilingual environment, this is abduction indeed.

Since Masako's marriage, her Sagittarian Sun has buckled under the pressure of the darkly Plutonic forces at the palace. Although Sagittarius is a fire sign, which suggests strength and resilience, it is also *mutable* and thus lacks the stubborn intensity of either Diana's fixed t-square or Gandhi's fixed opposition. When adversity strikes, there is not as much innate fighting power as with fixed and cardinal elements.

Enter Uranus

But wait—Uranus is involved here as well. When found in hard aspect to the Sun, there is a suggestion of a strong independent streak. Despite her illness (which we'll examine in more detail in the upcoming section on cardinal squares), and despite her apparent withdrawal from life, Masako is a rebel.

Alas, she has yet to own this energy. We do see it operating, though, in the guise of her devoted husband. In June of 2004, Prince Naruhito held an unprecedented press conference in which he lambasted the officials of the highly conservative Imperial Household Agency and held them responsible for his wife's condition.[8]

Not only were Imperial Household Agency officials implicated in the Prince's diatribe, but his parents, the Emperor and Empress of Japan, were as well. In effect, the Prince was using the media to communicate with his parents rather than approach them directly—a strategy that shocked many commentators in Japan. Indeed, Prince Naruhito made a drastic break from tradition when he blasted the courtiers for "nullifying her career, as well as her character."[9]

The Astrology of Transformation

All this is suggestive of the Sun-Uranus square in Masako's chart. Like the early days of Diana's marriage—before she integrated the Uranus energies into her personality—Masako has yet to own the power of her Uranus-Pluto conjunction. Either she will learn how to do this, or it will be done *to* her, and probably in the same darkly manipulative way that it has happened so far. Whether she's able to own the power of her Uranus-Pluto might well depend on how she handles another square in her chart: between Jupiter in Aries and Venus-Mercury-Mars in Capricorn.

The Cardinal Square: Jupiter in Aries and Venus-Mercury-Mars in Capricorn

Unlike Masako's mutable square, where the energies are projected onto other people, in the cardinal square they are manifested in terms of inner conflicts. On one side is Jupiter in Aries, an echo of the freedom-loving energy of her Sagittarian Sun. On the other are Mars, Mercury, and Venus in Capricorn, which are indicative of much more conservative tendencies. While many in Japan have criticized the secretive officials at the Imperial Household Agency for stifling Masako's personality, there is evidence that there is a part of the Princess's personality that is conservative as well. One old school chum said that Masako was "very much the traditional Japanese woman—unlikely to take initiative or stick her neck out."[10] This makes sense in terms of Masako's Capricorn planets.

Clearly, there is a conflict in this chart between the need for freedom (Sagittarius) and a profound sense of duty and tradition (Capricorn). One manifestation of this conflict is Masako's struggle with shingles and depression. Note that both are Capricornian ailments. (Saturn rules the skin and symbolizes depression.) It's no mistake that she started complaining of these symptoms when transiting Saturn opposed her Capricorn planets. Interestingly, Masako has also complained of dizziness, which would bring Jupiter in Aries (Aries ruling the head) into the picture as well.

The Astrology of Transformation

Masako is in a tough bind. She lives in a culture in which, to quote a popular Japanese saying, "the protruding nail gets pounded down." With her Sagittarius Sun squaring Uranus, and with Jupiter in Aries, she yearns to express herself and go her own way. But the dictates of the culture, as well as a highly conservative part of her own nature (Venus, Mars, and Mercury in Capricorn), militate against it—thus, her illness. Starting in late 2008, transiting Pluto will conjoin her Capricorn planets and transiting Saturn will square them. It might not be till then that the Princess is able to make any deep changes in her life.

---

1. *Diana: Queen of Hearts*, 1998 Hallmark documentary narrated by Richard Attenborough.

2. Alan Oken, *Alan Oken's Complete Astrology* (New York: Bantam Books, 1998), p. 396.

3. "Princess Diana: A Beautiful, Tragic Life Cut Short," *CNN.com*, August 31, 1997, http://edition.cnn.com/WORLD/9708/31/diana.life/index.html.

4. N. Onishi, "A Princess's Distress Pierces Japan's Veil of Secrecy," *New York Times*, August 7, 2004.

5. As this book went to press in September 2006, Princess Kiko, the wife of the current emperor's second son, gave birth to a baby boy, potentially resolving the royal family's succession crisis and taking pressure off Masako to produce a male heir to the throne.

6. A. Faiola, "Princess Masako Bears Royal Burden," *Washington Post*, June 25, 2004, p. 1.

7. *Mainichi Shimbun*, http://www.mainichi-msn.co.jp.

8. A. Faiola, "Princess Masako Bears Royal Burden," p. 1.

9. Ibid.

10. "Crown Princess Masako," *iKjeld.com*, http://www.ikjeld.com/files/biographies/princess_masako.html.

CHAPTER THREE

The Conjunction

- 0° hard aspect
- Keywords: intensity, focus

Conjunctions occur when two or more planets lie in close proximity. The conjunction is like a marriage: sometimes happy, sometimes not, but always integral. Venus and Jupiter conjoined are much happier bedfellows than Venus and Pluto (which we'll see with Katharine Graham); Moon and Venus are much happier than Moon and Uranus (Charles Schulz). When factoring signs into the equation, you have yet more potential combustion.

Whatever the signs, the yoking together of two or more archetypal forces tends to create vortex intensity and a you-can't-see-the-forest-for-the-trees blindness. For that reason, there is a greater danger that the chart as a whole will be thrown off balance, especially when there are incompatible planets involved. Indeed, the conjunction is one of the most powerful aspects in the zodiac. For that reason, it must be handled with great consciousness and care.

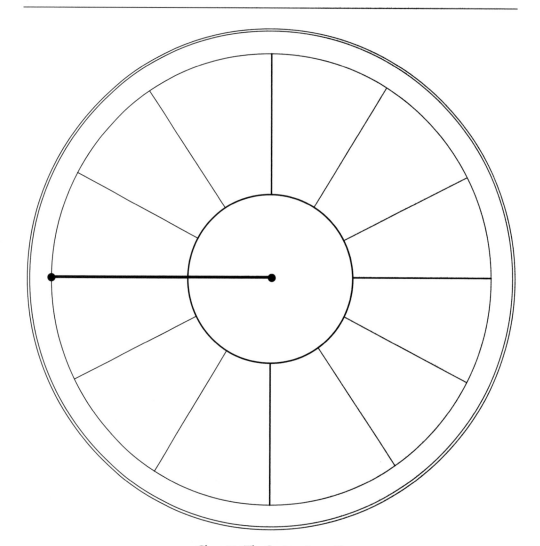

Chart 11: The Conjunction—0°

The Cardinal Conjunction: Katharine Graham

When Katharine Graham died in 2001, she was called one of the most influential women of her generation. As publisher of the *Washington Post*, Graham oversaw two groundbreaking stories in American journalism, the Pentagon Papers and the Watergate scandal, the second of which toppled the president of the United States. During her reign at the paper, Graham raised revenues twentyfold and transformed it from a relatively small family-owned business into a major corporation.[1]

But Kay Graham was not always a dynamic publisher and businesswoman. Soon after graduating from college in the 1930s, she married and became the prototypical housewife, cloistered in the family's farmhouse and bowing to her husband's every demand. It took two tragedies—her husband's psychosis and his subsequent suicide—to jolt her out of complacency. In 1997 she wrote *Personal History*, a Pulitzer Prize–winning memoir that tracks her evolution from doormat housewife to media mogul. Her life, one writer noted, is a "post feminist parable" for millions of women in their struggle for equality.

When Katharine Meyer was born on June 16, 1917, the planets most associated with femininity, Venus and the Moon, were paired with two of the most ruthless forces in the zodiac, Pluto and Uranus (chart 12). It's no surprise that Graham's transformation involved a total revamping of her identity as a woman. In this chapter we'll be focusing on the Venus-Pluto contact and how it helped shape her destiny.

Venus Conjunct Pluto in Cancer: All or Nothing at All

What comes to mind when you think of the astrological sign of Cancer? Home, family, and the need to nurture and be nurtured, right? How about Venus? The urge for intimacy and connection, and a striving for beauty and harmony are key concepts. With Venus in Cancer, issues relating to emotional closeness and security are brought to the fore. In this placement, one's sexuality is irrevocably linked to a deep need to feel safe. These are two energies that meld beautifully in an aspect.

Now how did Pluto ever get invited to this party?

The God from Hell (literally) was Katharine Graham's main challenge. So intense was the Venus-Pluto conjunction that for many years Katharine split it off from consciousness, retreating into the safe intellectualism of her Gemini planets.

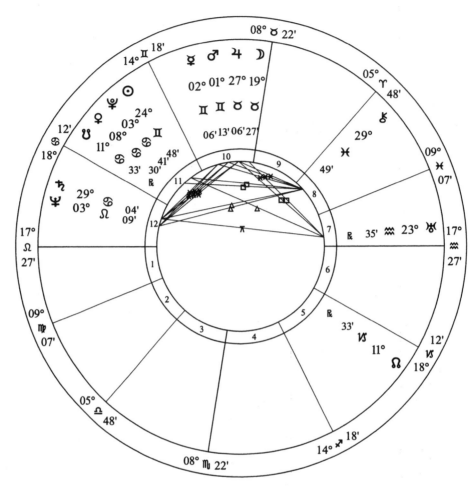

Chart 12: Katharine Graham
June 16, 1917 / 8:43 a.m. EST
New York, New York / Placidus houses

And who can blame her? The Venus-Pluto combination is not easy. Venus likes everything to be beautiful and harmonious. Along with Jupiter and the Moon, it is one of the places of refuge in a chart: spaces within ourselves where we go to get balanced and to feel at ease. What happens when you discover that that safe, peaceful territory has been invaded by a force that won't rest until it has dredged up every unsavory memory, every shameful experience and impulse that you've so carefully kept hidden away?

You run in terror is what you do. But as we all know (astrologers more than most), you can run but you can't hide. There, in the eleventh house of Katharine's chart, sat Pluto like a time bomb, waiting to explode.

In the next section we'll examine the chain of events that led to her husband's suicide, and to Katharine Graham's subsequent transformation into one of the most powerful women on the planet.

The Astrology of Transformation

Despite the need for intimacy represented by Venus in Cancer and Moon in Taurus (especially strong here because they are in mutual reception), Graham grew up in emotional isolation. She came of age on an immense estate in New York called Mount Kisco. Her father, Eugene Meyer, had amassed a fortune by his early thirties. In 1933 he bought the *Washington Post*, a fledgling enterprise with dim prospects, and became publisher. So busy and influential were Eugene and his wife, Agnes, that they were away for months at a time, leaving Katharine and her siblings in the care of an assortment of servants and nannies.[2]

Katharine's response to this was to deny her need for intimacy and retreat into the safe haven of her Gemini planets: excelling at school, reading, and developing a lively interest in politics and current events.

Having numbed her deep need for connection, Katharine now had to do something to de-anesthetize herself. And what better way than by creating a pantheon out of her powerful family? We first see this vis-à-vis her relationships with her elder siblings, and later through her idealization of her mother, who became the personification of beauty and intelligence. Agnes Meyer was a daunting figure in her own right—the confidante of Thomas Mann, Adlai Stevenson, and other prominent figures of the day. Katharine took this grandiose picture and blew it up into even larger proportions—projecting all the intensity of her Venus-Pluto conjunction onto these family (Cancer) members.

Once Katharine had learned to project Venus-Pluto onto others, it was easy to replicate this pattern with her husband, Philip Graham, the man who would take over at the *Washington Post*. As was the case with her family, Phil became the carrier of this intense energy, relieving Katharine of that responsibility.

Phil was a perfect illustration of her Venus-Pluto complex. One of Katharine's first encounters with her husband-to-be took place at a party at which her older sister Bis was present. As Katharine sat in the corner watching her vaunted sibling, Phil watched Katharine.

Noticing her ambivalence, he leaned over and said, with a twinkle in his eyes, "Are we for her or against her?" Here was a man she barely knew, articulating something that she had barely admitted to herself.[3]

I challenge anyone to find a more incisive description of the Venus-Pluto dynamic: the urge for intimacy shot through with Plutonic intensity. The Cancerian element is beautifully brought out in Katharine's complicated feelings about her sister. From the beginning, Katharine knew she had met an extraordinary man.

After they were married, Katharine's deification of her husband intensified. Phil was the godhead around which everything else revolved. Graham doted on her husband and acquiesced to him in everything she did.

Not surprisingly, as Phil's power expanded, Katharine's shrank. She increasingly became the target of Phil's jokes. He took to calling her "porky" and making her the butt of jokes. The final straw came with an ill-conceived financial arrangement in which Katharine agreed to pay all monthly expenses out of her share of the Meyer family fortune so that Phil would have enough money to buy the majority of *Washington Post* stock from her parents. This is one of the shadow manifestations of a hard aspect between Venus and Pluto: a polarization between power and powerlessness, with each person assuming the corresponding roles of victim-perpetrator.[4]

The fact that Katharine gave so much of her power to this man was not a healthy situation. While her self-esteem dwindled, Phil developed a case of hubris that would have shocked Zeus. He was drinking and getting into wild, irrational rages at parties. The pièce de résistance came in the early 1960s when Phil took to berating President Kennedy.

In 1958, Philip Graham had a nervous breakdown. In 1963, after years of struggling with undiagnosed bipolar disorder, he took a 28-gauge shotgun off the rack at the family farm and went into the bathroom and killed himself.

After several weeks of numb disbelief, Katharine pulled herself together and resolved to take over at the *Washington Post*. She had none of the credentials necessary for such a mammoth undertaking—she couldn't understand a balance sheet or follow even the most rudimentary financial discussions. But with the help of Sun, Mercury, and Mars in Gemini (a love of learning, a facility for language, and a knack for networking and bringing people together), she slowly learned the ropes.

Another part of her transformation from mousy housewife to media magnate involved the alchemization of her Venus-Pluto conjunction. Where before she played the powerless victim, she now became one of the most powerful women in the country. It's a bit ironic that, when it came time to hand over the paper to her son, it became impossible for her to relinquish control. Ironic, but not difficult to understand—not with Venus-Pluto. Where before she'd had little or no power, now she demanded it all.

However, the story of Kate Graham's transformation is not all about power and control. Another aspect was the way she accessed the Cancerian energies in her chart and redefined what it was to nurture and be nurtured. Where before this had been done solely in the context of family life, she now transferred that warm, feminine energy to the workplace, becoming an able and caring administrator and publisher.

The Mutable Conjunction: Charles Schulz

Probably no single human being, with the possible exception of Walt Disney, had a greater impact on the pop-culture landscape of the twentieth century than Charles Schulz. The creator of the beloved *Peanuts* comic strip gave us the hapless Charlie Brown, tart-tongued Lucy, and lovable Snoopy.

The only child of a Midwestern barber, Schulz had a syndicated column by the time he was twenty-eight and a sprawling estate complete with a miniature golf course before he turned forty. At the time of his death, he boasted 355 million readers in seventy-five countries.

Yet for all his success, Schulz was a man beset by melancholy. He was also prone to panic attacks, often finding it difficult to venture out into public places. In this chapter we'll examine the role his mutable Moon-Uranus conjunction played in his life (chart 13).

Moon Conjunct Uranus in Pisces:
Electrifier of the Imagination, Harbinger of Separation

In some ways this combination creates a dynamic similar to that of Katharine Graham's conjunction: an unruly planet (Uranus), placed in an empathetic water sign (Pisces), conjunct an empathetic planet (the Moon). However, there are two big differences. First, the lightning imagination of Uranus is much more comfortable in the dreamy waters of Pisces than Pluto could ever hope to be in home-loving Cancer. Second, Schulz's conjunction was

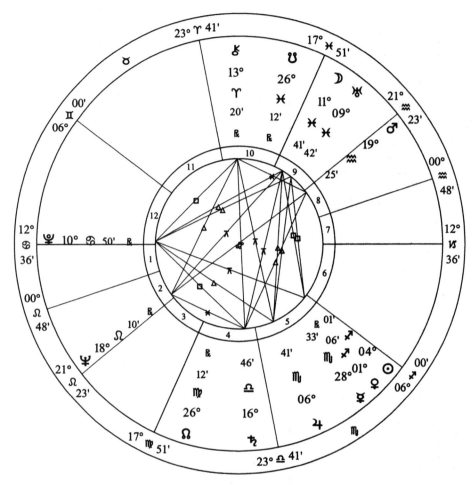

Chart 13: Charles Schulz
November 26, 1922 / 7:07 p.m. CST
St. Paul, Minnesota / Placidus houses

mutable, and Graham's was cardinal. The very nature of cardinal signs is change—sometimes abrupt—on both the inner and outer levels. This set the stage for a series of traumatic disruptions in her life.

Schulz's mutable conjunction, on the other hand, created a much more fluid environment. One commentator noted how Schulz's history of "slights, hurts, resentments, and failures" fueled his art.[5] However, unlike Graham, the wounding Schulz experienced as a result of those slights never disrupted his routine. It informed his drawings—Charlie Brown, the perennial loser, was Schulz's alter ego, after all—but never upset the apple cart of his psyche.

This is not to say there were not upsets. There were indeed—there almost *had* to be, given the disparate energies involved. The biggest one was a searing rejection from the love of his life—in the same year his comic strip was syndicated. Years after the rejection, Schulz would recall it as if it had occurred yesterday.

Alchemy or Not: The Astrology of Transformation

Thanks to the alchemizing power of Moon-Uranus in Pisces, this too became grist for the mill. The rejection, by an auburn-haired beauty named Donna Johnson, was the inspiration for the "Little Red-Haired Girl," Charlie Brown's unrequited love.

Indeed, all sorts of real-life elements were alchemized into art thanks to Schulz's mutable conjunction. So personal were the Peanuts characters that many commentators have said that the comic strip was like Schulz's diary. Lucy was based on his irascible daughter Meredith, and when his son started taking helicopter lessons, Schulz drew Snoopy's ears twirling around like rotors.[6]

Let us not forget that Uranus is the great revolutionary. The mysticism and fantasy of mutable Pisces are supercharged by the electrical energies of this planet. "There used to be so many taboo things in cartoons, and he blasted that to smithereens," said Rheta Grimsley Johnson, his biographer.[7]

"He used the strip as therapy," said Chris Brown, another comic-strip artist. "He reached down into the muck of his own soul and came up with diamonds."[8]

The Fixed Conjunction: Martha Stewart

She has been called America's hostess. She combines the "beauty of the orchid with the efficiency of a computer." Her books and magazines have more than twenty-five million readers worldwide, and her television programs are almost as successful. She is Martha Stewart, and despite her past legal and financial difficulties, one gets the sense that she is here to stay.[9]

She came from humble beginnings. Born Martha Kostyra to working-class Polish-American parents, she did the usual things that American girls do—learning cooking and homemaking from her mother and gardening from her perfectionist father.

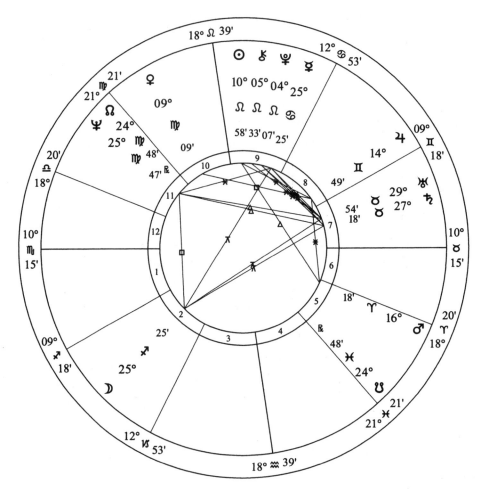

Chart 14: Martha Stewart
August 3, 1941 / 1:33 p.m. EDT
Jersey City, New Jersey / Placidus houses

But she was clearly not your usual American girl. From a young age she exhibited the leadership gifts of her Leo Sun (exalted in the ninth house, just 8° from the Midheaven). When she was ten, she started to do "extra-special things" on babysitting jobs to earn money. Before long, she was organizing neighborhood birthday parties. Her first catering job was making breakfast for the football team at Nutley High School. Later, when she was a housewife in an upscale Connecticut suburb, she started giving cooking lessons in her kitchen for neighborhood children. The Leo flair was in evidence there as well. "I gave them chef's hats and they learned to cook omelets," she said.[10]

As her reputation and business skills grew, she rented space and opened a gourmet food shop. We get an inkling of the intensity of Sun conjunct Pluto when Stewart started a catering service with a friend. Her buddy quit after a year, saying she didn't want to work "128 hours a week."[11] In 1977 a new company, Martha Stewart, Inc., was born, and in 1982 she published her first book to rave reviews.

Other books followed, each with a publicity tour and a growing number of fans. In the late '80s she added a new line for Kmart, signing on to a five-year, $5 million contract. The same year, her husband left her, weary of the Sun-Pluto whirlwind.

Let's take a more careful look at this planetary combination and see how it has contributed to her astounding success.

Sun Conjunct Pluto in Leo: Illegal Hormone of the Astrological World

If people knew the power of this conjunction, it would be banned. Lance Armstrong, the seven-time winner of the Tour de France, also has it, although in Virgo.

Sun-Pluto combinations indicate a usurping of the will. The Sun, symbol of the life force, is "abducted" by Pluto, lord of the underworld. Someone with Sun in hard aspect to Pluto is likely to experience a radical redefinition of identity at some point in life. Unlike the square, Pluto in conjunction is less likely to be projected outward. The abductors more typically manifest as inner drives that hijack the life in some way. As a result, the ensuing changes appear to unfold organically (but with high drama) in the life of the native.

There have been a number of Plutonic transformations in Martha Stewart's life. While still in college, she worked as a model, flying to Paris on several occasions. At nineteen, she became engaged to Andrew Stewart and dropped out of school. Within a year she was back at school, and soon gave birth to their first and only child. In the early years of her marriage she became a stockbroker, working fourteen-hour days and making $100,000 a year. When the market dried up, she quit her job and returned to homemaking. From there, the Martha Phenomenon grew steadily: a home-based gourmet business, her first book, and the whirlwind that has become Martha Stewart Living Omnimedia.[12]

Looking at all this in retrospect, each of these transformations seems reasonable, even logical. Her modeling experience helped develop Martha's innate artistry and her Leonine love of theater. Her work as a stockbroker laid the groundwork for the megabusiness that was to follow. It all fits together, like interlocking pieces of a puzzle.

But Sun-Pluto is never easy. Imagine the disorientation that a nineteen-year-old college student feels at leaving behind all her friends and perhaps even her academic career—what did she know at that time? Imagine the shock of going from stockbroker to suburban housewife, and then the angst she must have felt when indicted on four counts and sentenced to five months in prison. Each of these represented the tearing down of a painstakingly erected identity. The last one, in particular, was an abduction of mythic proportions. When in the throes of a Plutonic "death," no one really believes that rebirth will follow.

This is remarkably similar to the changes Lance Armstrong has undergone in his short life. At age twenty-five, he was on the verge of breaking into the top five in international rankings, only to be diagnosed with a life-threatening cancer. His recovery led to the Lance Armstrong Foundation and, most recently, his spectacular seventh win at the Tour de France.

Lance's transformations were played out against a Virgo backdrop—dire illness, service, and the precise calculations that enabled his victories in France.

For Martha Stewart, the stage was set in brilliant Leo colors: the sumptuous layouts of her magazines and books, the muted colors and paisleys of her sheets and pillowcases.

Unlike Princess Masako's Sun-Pluto square, where the abductors took the form of the bureaucrats of the Imperial Household Agency, Martha's changes were initiated from within. She decided, on her own free will, to get married at age nineteen. She made the decision to quit her high-paying job as a stockbroker and resume her life as a housewife and mother. True, the upheaval created by her indictment was clearly instigated by outside forces, but it was prompted by her own behavior.

The Astrology of Transformation

Transformation is "built into" hard Pluto aspects, and Martha Stewart has already undergone numerous reincarnations in her life.

The question is, where will she go from here? What has she learned from her five months in prison? Like Princess Masako, we have not yet seen the last act of this drama.

The answering of this question will be postponed till we look at yet another dynamic of Martha Stewart's chart—a trine between a ruling Leo Sun and a headstrong Mars in Aries. This is the real litmus test for Stewart. How she handles that will ultimately determine whether she's able to learn from past mistakes.

1. M. Berger, "Katharine Graham of Washington Post Dies at 84," *New York Times*, July 18, 2001, p. 1.

2. Carol Felsenthal, *Power, Privilege, and the Post: The Katharine Graham Story* (New York: Seven Stories Press, 1993).

3. Katharine Graham, *Personal History* (New York: Vintage Books, 1998), p. 109.

4. Melissa Burdick Harmon, "The Transformation of Katharine Graham," *Biography*, March 2003, p. 92.

5. P. Chin, "Gentle Genius," *People*, February 28, 2000, pp. 54–59.

6. Ibid.

7. Ibid.

8. Ibid.

9. Virginia Meachum, *Martha Stewart: Successful Businesswoman* (Berkeley Heights, NJ: Enslow Publishers, 1998), p. 94.

10. Ibid., p. 14.

11. Ibid., p. 28.

12. Ibid., p. 30.

PART TWO

Working with Soft Aspects

CHAPTER FOUR

The Trine

- 120° soft aspect
- Same elements

The components of a trine are like the ingredients of a recipe: they all meld together into a harmonious whole. However, like the high caloric content of desserts, it's easy to overdo, especially if sweet, creamy icings (Jupiter and Venus, for example) are part of the package. When Uranus and Pluto are involved, the dish is likely to be a lot more spicy.

Whatever the ingredients, one must be on guard against inflation. Precisely because the soft aspects are so easy, one is lulled into a false sense of complacency. This is all the more true if elevated and/or dignified planets are involved. In this chapter we'll see how each of the following people dealt with the deceptively easy energy of the trine.

The Fire Trine: Martha Stewart

In this chapter we return to Martha Stewart, the one-woman industry who was the focus of a lengthy federal investigation (chart 16). We'll examine how a powerful trine between Sun and Mars contributed to her incredible success but also fanned the flames that led to her troubles.

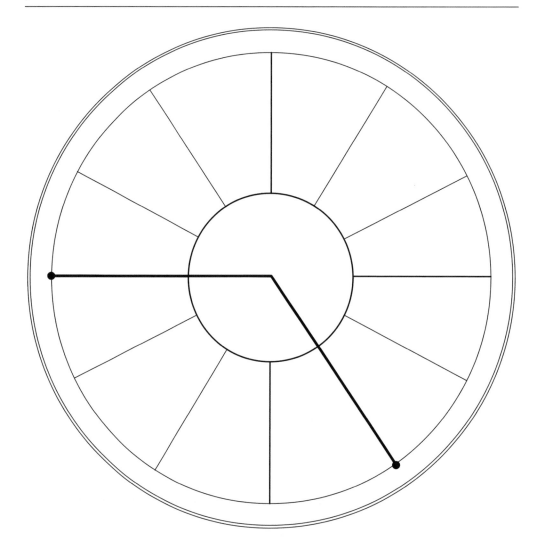

Chart 15: The Trine—120°

It's curious to learn that this powerhouse, one with so much yang energy in her chart (Sun, Moon, and Mars in fire signs), decided to marry at age nineteen. This is especially perplexing given the fact that so many career-minded women put off marriage or reject it altogether. What could ambitious Martha Kostyra have been thinking when she decided to tie the knot before she'd even graduated from college?

What that clever girl was thinking (although probably not consciously) was that she needed the support system that only an intelligent, ambitious husband could provide to realize her dreams. The time was the early '60s—before most women had reaped the benefits of the women's movement. Like Mozart and other eighteenth-century composers who solicited the support of patron-kings, Martha sized up the situation and knew that she could not go it alone—at least not at first.

Sun in Leo Trine Mars in Aries

Both the Sun and Mars are in ruling signs. The Sun is in dynamic Leo, the archetypal king. It is bolstered by Mars, the mythic warrior, at the height of his power in Aries. A planet in its own sign is like a ruler in its own country—supremely powerful. Martha Stewart has been likened to a bullet in flight, a perfect image for the synergy created between these two planets. Mars in Aries is the enabler who implements the grandiose plans of Martha's ruling Sun.

This formidable trine is bolstered by an intense Sun-Pluto conjunction. In addition, the Sun is the most elevated planet in the chart, just 8° from the Midheaven. We've already seen some of the manifestations of this astrological combination in the guise of Stewart's hugely successful businesses.

It's also interesting to note how the Leonine flair for drama is expressed in Stewart's life. This has been true throughout her career—from the chef hats she gave to neighborhood kids in her first cooking classes to the critical success of her first book, praised for its theatrical packaging. This is close to the way Stewart herself describes her mission. "Entertaining," she says, is an opportunity to express "warmth, individuality, and personal taste"—perfect Leo characteristics![1]

For all the energy and verve on display, one wonders if it isn't too much of a good thing. Indeed, Martha Stewart has always had a propensity to overdo, and to sacrifice detail in order to achieve her goals. Shortly after her first books were published, charges of plagiarism surfaced.[2] She either didn't notice, or conveniently forgot, that she'd lifted material from other

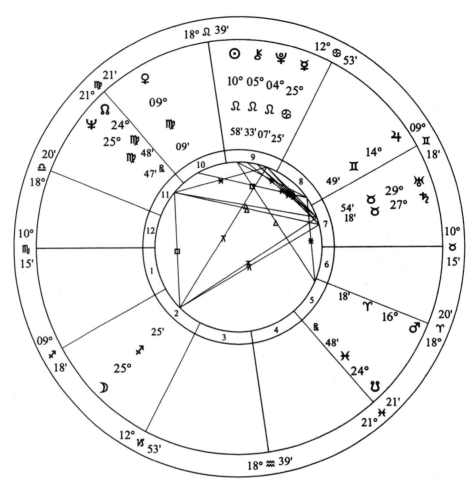

Chart 16: Martha Stewart
August 3, 1941 / 1:33 p.m. EDT
Jersey City, New Jersey / Placidus houses

sources. In addition, critics have cited the unrealistic expectations Stewart puts on readers. Her timetables, said one, are "really impossible."[3] And this does not even mention the morass she found herself in after being charged with insider trading.

But Martha, as always, is not one to be cowed. On the day before she was sentenced in 2004, she was seen out on the town, partying with movie stars and other celebs.[4] We'll explore ways in which Stewart could provide a counterweight to these inflationary energies in the sections on the semisquare and sesquiquadrate in chapter 11.

The Air Trine: Rush Limbaugh and Jane Fonda

Here we have a contrastive study in ideological inflation vis-à-vis two people from opposite ends of the political spectrum: Rush Limbaugh, renowned for his right-wing radio rants, and Jane Fonda, an Academy Award–winning actress who was a strident antiwar activist during the 1960s. Both have prominent Mars-led air trines in their charts. We'll see how the trines helped energize their personalities but also contributed to some unfortunate outcomes.

Rush Limbaugh

Born on January 12, 1951 (chart 17), Limbaugh has Sun in Capricorn and Aquarius rising—polar energies that suggest a conflict between a need to uphold the status quo (Capricorn) and the urge to blaze new trails (Ascendant, Venus, and Mars in Aquarius). We can see both sides in his radio persona: Limbaugh's rants are directed against the left-wing "establishment" he believes has overrun American culture (thus seeing himself as an Aquarian revolutionary intent upon dethroning the liberal powers that be). However, he ultimately wants to return to what he sees as the bedrock values of America's founding fathers—a manifestation of Capricornian conservatism.

Limbaugh was born to a well-to-do Midwestern family, the son of a lawyer and a Republican committeewoman. He was an unpopular child who later dropped out of college. He was fired from several jobs before taking a job with a radio station in California, where he was lauded for his ad-libbing irreverence. Liberals accuse him of weaving fact with fiction during his radio broadcasts; indeed, many dubious statements have emanated from his lips. Regarding the women's movement: "Women were doing quite well in this country before feminism came along." On Native Americans: "There are more American Indians alive today than there were when Columbus arrived or at any other time in history. Does this sound like a record of genocide?"[5]

What fuels these inflammatory proclamations? A trine between Mars and Neptune in his chart provides one clue.

Mars in Aquarius Trine Neptune in Libra

Aquarius is a fixed air sign ruled by Uranus. It is both stubborn and iconoclastic, two qualities that are readily apparent in Limbaugh. Neptune in Libra trines his first-house Mars, infusing it with idealism. Although Limbaugh poses as a political pundit, he has the aura of a religious crusader propagating Republican values with messianic intensity.

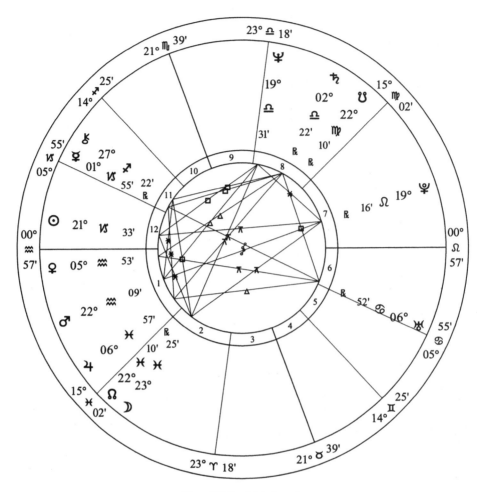

Chart 17: Rush Limbaugh
January 12, 1951 / 7:50 a.m. CST
Cape Girardeau, Missouri / Placidus houses

Given the involvement of Neptune, it's also interesting to note Limbaugh's well-publicized addiction to pain killers, and this despite his diatribes against irresponsible drug addicts and the wasteful welfare programs meant to reform them. Here we see inflationary rhetoric combined with Neptunian escapism, a combination that has not served him well. Although the Mars-Neptune trine certainly contributes to his charisma, it also generates a rather bombastic communication style that alienates as many people as it seduces.[6]

Jane Fonda

Jane Fonda is a legendary screen actress who has reinvented herself a number of times throughout her career. From the sexpot image of her early films to her more weighty roles (she won Academy Awards for *Klute* and *Coming Home*), she has kept her fans guessing. In later years she abandoned acting to start a lucrative aerobics business. She ultimately jettisoned that for a more traditional housewife role after her marriage to Ted Turner. Her latest transformation involved a conversion to fundamentalist Christianity.

Fonda is most remembered for her antiwar and antiestablishment activism of the 1960s, a time when she infuriated conservatives with trips to North Vietnam and assertions that U.S. soldiers in Vietnam were "war criminals." It is during this time that we can most clearly see the inflationary tendencies of her Mars-Chiron trine (chart 18).[7]

Mars in Aquarius Trine Chiron in Gemini

Like Rush Limbaugh, Fonda has Mars in the fixed air sign of Aquarius. As we've seen, this can denote a stubborn, crusading quality, which in Fonda's case has expressed itself through extreme left-wing ideologies. Because of her fiery nature (she has Sun in Sagittarius and Moon in Leo), this took on some rather dramatic manifestations. One example is the time she sat atop an antiaircraft carrier during her 1972 trip to North Vietnam (one used to shoot down American planes) and posed for the cameras. Fonda later spearheaded a chain of "F.T.A." (F*** the Army) coffeehouses outside American military bases, encouraging soldiers to desert. After her return from North Vietnam, she insisted that no U.S. prisoners of war were being hurt or tortured, only to have those assertions flatly contradicted one year later by returning Vietnam vets. She called them "hypocrites and liars."[8]

The inflationary tendencies of Fonda's Mars-Chiron trine are aggravated by conflicts with her father, shown through Mars's rulership of her fourth house as well as a Sun-Saturn square. The relationship was known to be a tense one.

Years later, Fonda reflected on her behavior. "It hurt so many soldiers," she said of her support for the Viet Cong. "It galvanized such hostility. It was the most horrible thing I could possibly have done. It was just thoughtless."[9]

One wonders whether Rush Limbaugh will ever gain such perspective on his Mars-Neptune trine.

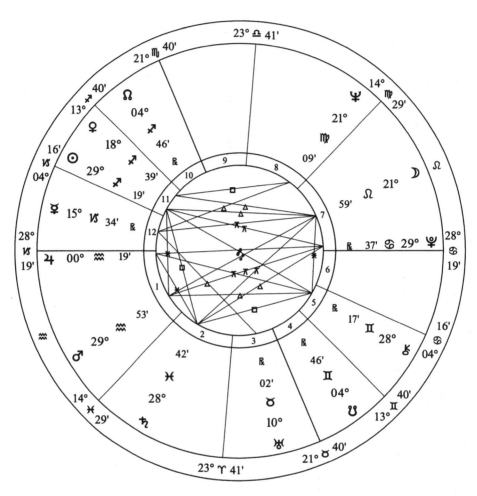

Chart 18: Jane Fonda
December 21, 1937 / 9:14 a.m. EST
Manhattan, New York / Placidus houses

The Water Trine: Kurt Cobain

For many, Kurt Cobain has become synonymous with the pain and dislocation of the latch-key generation: children of broken homes left to fend for themselves during the lonely years of adolescence. Born in 1967 to a working-class family, Cobain's parents divorced when he was eight. He said he never felt loved or secure after that.

Cobain was a misfit at high school. "I got beat up a lot," he said. He identified with gays and students of color at the school, rejecting the mainstream culture.[10]

After dropping out of school, he started playing in bands in the Seattle area. In 1988 he formed Nirvana, the grunge group that would revolutionize rock music. "Grunge," said one writer, "is what happens when children of divorce get their hands on guitars." Cobain "reminded his peers they were not alone."[11]

However, despite three dignified planets and a chart comprised mostly of trines and sextiles, Cobain himself was very much alone (chart 19). Perhaps to offset his alienation, he married singer Courtney Love and had a child by age twenty-five. Two years later, Cobain killed himself.

Mars in Scorpio Trine Sun in Pisces

Cobain had eight out of ten planets in water—nine if you count Chiron. Two of the eight, Mars and Sun, are in an exact trine.

Most people would consider a close trine between the Sun and Mars an asset. The Sun is the life force, and Mars the actuator of the Sun's energies. With an exact trine between the two—and Mars dignified in Scorpio—it's easy to imagine the benefits this planetary connection could bring.

This aspect was certainly an asset in terms of Cobain's musical career, and particularly his stage persona. His electrifying performances were a byproduct of that dynamic trine (although Pluto and Uranus conjunct the Ascendant didn't hurt, either).

But let's look at this trine in the context of his chart. There are two big problems with this lovely 120° aspect. As already noted, Cobain had eight planets in water. There are no planets in air or fire. Right from the start, there is imbalance. Right from the start, we know there is too much yin energy for this person's good.

In addition, there is a preponderance of "soft" aspects. Cobain's chart is comprised of two grand trines in water—one very tight, one quite loose. Grand trines are wonderful for infusing a chart with energy and confidence, but they also create the potential for overkill. Because of the lack of hard aspects and the predominance of water, Kurt Cobain was an exceedingly vulnerable individual, one with very few of the defenses needed in a competitive, fast-paced world.

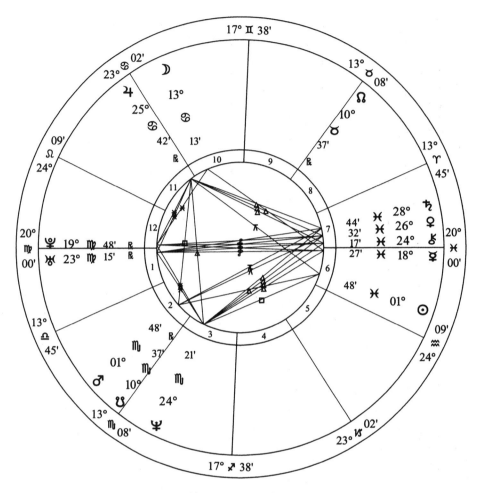

Chart 19: Kurt Cobain
February 20, 1967 / 7:20 p.m. PST
Aberdeen, Washington / Placidus houses

The Sun-Mars trine aggravated the elemental imbalance by adding to the total number of planets in water. At the same time, though, because Mars is involved, Cobain made a desperate attempt to fight back.

Cobain had many "'weapons" in his watery Sun-Mars arsenal. First and foremost was Nirvana, the group that brought him fame and fortune. It's no coincidence that the group was started the year that both Cobain's solar arc Sun and Mars hit the angles of his chart. Cobain's parents couldn't understand his desire to drop out of school and start a rock band.

"To them," Cobain said, "I was wasting my life. To me, I was fighting for it."[12] On the dark side, heroin also acted as a mode of defense, something he called his "shield." His brief career was also punctuated by provocative acts of rebellion against the very musical establishment that made him rich and famous, such as the time he showed up for a photo shoot at *Rolling Stone* magazine wearing a t-shirt saying "CORPORATE MAGAZINES STILL SUCK."[13]

Finally—and tragically—there was his affinity for guns, the quintessential symbol of phallic Mars energy. It was with a gun that he ended his life on April 5, 1994. "It was clear," said a writer from *Newsweek* several weeks after Cobain's death, "that what Nirvana's singer really needed protection from was himself."[14]

The Earth Trine: Katharine Hepburn

Here we have another legendary screen star: a feminist way before her time who took to wearing pants, challenging studio heads, and playing brassy roles that few others would consider. Katharine Hepburn is the only woman to have won four Academy Awards, three of them after she was sixty. "I lived my life like a man," she admitted. "I've been as terrified as the next person, but you've got to keep a-goin'."[15]

It's strange to think of this woman, with a Sun-Moon conjunction in conservative Taurus, as a revolutionary force in American culture (chart 20). On closer inspection, though, one discovers several trines between that cautious Sun and a Mars-Uranus conjunction in Capricorn. Let's look more closely at how this aspect created inflationary tendencies, as well as how it provided the sustaining energy for her independent life.

Mars-Uranus (Conjunct) in Capricorn Trine Sun-Mercury in Taurus

This aspect mixes the stability and conservatism of two earth signs with the electrical energies of a Mars-Uranus conjunction. The conjunction of Mars and Uranus endows the native with tremendous willpower and persistence. Combined with the trines to both the Sun and Mercury, it gave Hepburn the courage she needed to go head to head with studio execs and forge her way in the world. No doubt the energy of this trine also gave Hepburn the power to bounce back from adversity (she was called "box office poison" by one critic in the early years of her career).[16]

While creating great tenacity and willpower, this combination also generates a great deal of nervous tension, and perhaps just a bit too much courage. Once, when the filming

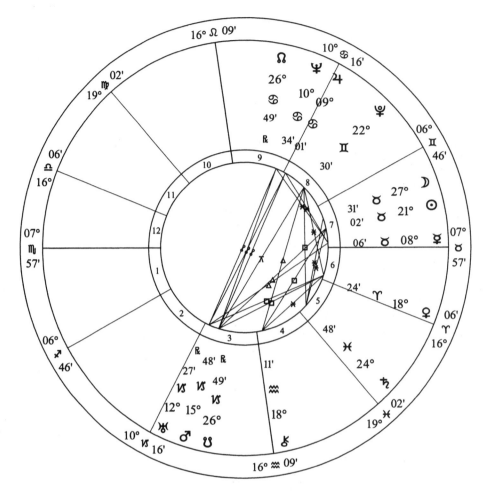

Chart 20: Katharine Hepburn
May 12, 1907 / 5:47 p.m. EST
Hartford, Connecticut / Placidus houses

on one of her movies went one day over schedule, the largely unknown twenty-six-year-old actress charged the studio $10,000. "Shame on you, Kathy," Hepburn said of her behavior many years later. The powers that be eventually got even with her, demanding she pay $14,000 to buy herself out of a disastrous theatrical production that was ruining what remained of her reputation.[17]

One of the most interesting facets of this aspect is that the Mars-Uranus conjunction falls in the third house—the domain of siblings. When Hepburn was fourteen, her older brother Tom hanged himself. Katharine was the first to find him. The young Kate, a tomboy who revered her brother, was devastated. For many years, Hepburn gave her brother's birthday as her own—creating great confusion for astrologers and biographers alike.

Many of the roles she played were fiercely loyal woman who stood up for the people they loved. She manifested this same loyalty in her life. Katharine couldn't save her brother from a tragic and premature death, but she hung on tooth and nail as Spencer Tracy, her lover of twenty-six years, went on one alcoholic binge after another. She also endured numerous affairs the actor had during their relationship, as well as his refusal to divorce his wife.

In Hepburn's case, the inflationary tendencies of the trine took the form of unbridled loyalty—viewed as inappropriate by some. The great actress would sit on the set and knit while Tracy filmed his scenes. She would curl up and sleep outside his hotel room where he'd barricaded himself while on one of his binges. Here is the staying power of Sun, Moon, and Mercury in Taurus combined with the inflationary tendencies of the trine to Mars-Uranus.

Unlike others engulfed by the inflation and excess energy of easy aspects and dignified planets, Hepburn never lost her balance. For all the ups and downs of her career, she lived life in a sure-footed manner, never succumbing to the perils of alcohol or other addictive substances. She died a death of natural causes, surrounded by friends and family.

1. Virginia Meachum, *Martha Stewart: Successful Businesswoman* (Berkeley Heights, NJ: Enslow Publishers, 1998), p. 38.

2. Ibid., p. 40.

3. Ibid., p. 44.

4. C. Hays and D. Carr, "Before Facing Judge, Stewart Is Out and About," business section, *New York Times*, July 15, 2004, p. 1.

5. "The Way Things Aren't: Rush Limbaugh Debates Reality," *FAIR*, March 8, 1992, http://www.fair.org/index.php?page=1895.

6. "Rush Limbaugh," *IMDb*, http://www.imdb.com/name/nm0510754.

7. "Jane Fonda," *IMDb*, http://www.imdb.com/name/nm0000404.

8. Ibid.

9. Ibid.

10. J. Giles, "The Poet of Alienation," *Newsweek*, April 18, 1994, pp. 33–38.

11. Ibid.

12. Ibid.

13. Ibid.

14. J. Giles, "The Poet of Alienation," pp. 33–38.

15. Katharine Hepburn, host, *All About Me*, video directed by David Heeley (Turner Pictures, 1992).

16. Ibid.

17. Ibid.

CHAPTER FIVE

The Sextile

- 30° soft aspect
- Compatible elements: fire/air, earth/water

The sextile is like a harmonious relationship between a brother and sister: they are members of the same family (i.e., compatible elemental pairings) but have different genders (fire versus air, earth versus water). The sextile doesn't have quite the punch of a trine, but it affords the same easy, flowing energy—and the same potential for complacency. In the following chapters we'll see how too many soft aspects, especially when combined with dignified planets, can lead to inflation and a crash landing with reality.

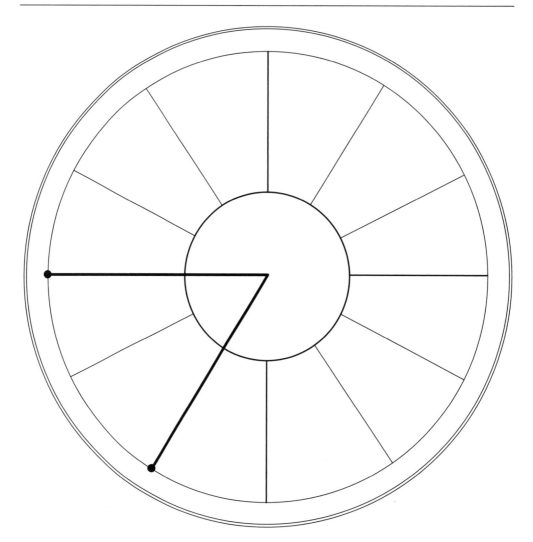

Chart 21: The Sextile—60°

John Nash

There was a grand ball in the town, and Karen was invited. She looked at the red shoes and put them on, thinking there was no harm in that. And then she went to the ball and commenced to dance. But when she wanted to go to the right, the shoes danced to the left, and when she wanted to dance up the room, the shoes danced down the room, down the stairs through the street, and out through the gates of the town. She danced, and was obliged to dance, far out into the dark wood. She was frightened, and wanted to throw the red shoes away; but they stuck fast. She tore off her stockings, but the shoes had grown fast to her feet. She danced and was obliged to go on dancing over field and meadow, in rain and sunshine, by night and by day.

—From *The Red Shoes* by Hans Christian Andersen

Nobel Prize winner John Nash is known as much for his groundbreaking achievements in mathematics as for his battle with schizophrenia. The subject of Ron Howard's 2001 film *A Beautiful Mind*, Nash spent the prime of his life in obscurity. After publishing several brilliant papers in his twenties, the West Virginia-born academic spent the next two decades in and out of mental health institutions. It wasn't till he was sixty-six that he won the Nobel.

John Forbes Nash Jr. was born on June 13, 1928, in Bluefield, West Virginia (chart 22). He had an independent and loving mother and a caring but emotionally remote father. There was nothing in his upbringing that suggested the now-discredited model of schizophrenia as resulting from childhood trauma or abuse. On the contrary, his mother and father, while flawed, provided a stable home for their son.

From the beginning, John Nash exhibited an unconventional intelligence that was marked by dramatic hunches and irascible eccentricity—both hallmarks of a strong Uranus. This is no surprise given that planet's elevated placement in his tenth house. Before we get to that, let's examine the sextiles in his chart. We'll see how they provided much of the motive force of his life, as well as being one of the prime instigators of the disease that nearly destroyed him.[1]

Sextiles and the Problem of Inflation

Nash has Sun conjunct Venus in Gemini sextile a Moon-Mars conjunction in Aries. There's also a wide sextile (10°) between Venus and Uranus.

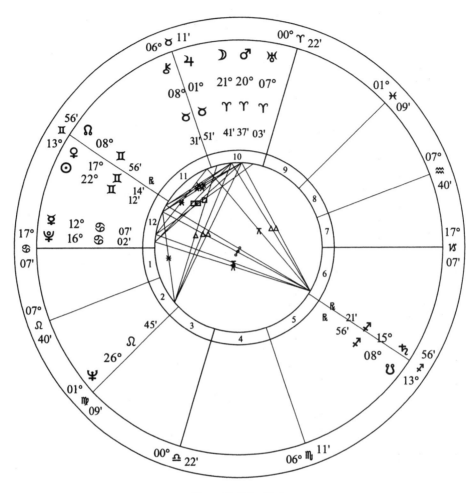

Chart 22: John Nash
June 13, 1928 / 7:00 a.m. EST
Bluefield, West Virginia / Placidus houses

In these aspects we find mutable air and cardinal fire, two masculine elements that indicate an outgoing, action-oriented temperament. Because both the Sun and Moon are involved, we know these aspects play a central role in Nash's life.

Gemini denotes a love of language and logic. Aries indicates a martial, self-centered individual possessing the ego needed to push through the myriad ideas generated by the Gemini Sun and Venus. The Aries energy is especially strong because Mars, its ruler, is located there. The Aries planets are the most exalted in the chart, giving them additional power.

In this configuration we see a whirlwind of energy: fanned by air, charged by Mars, and empowered by the Uranus-Midheaven conjunction—the astrological equivalent of inflation. Like the red shoes in the Hans Christian Andersen fairy tale, this inflated element can create a lot of havoc. The energy of Nash's sextiles is heightened by the fact that Mars disposits all the Aries planets.

This supercharged sextile complex had dire repercussions for three areas of Nash's life: his career, social life, and mental health. We'll see how all three are integrally connected.

Let's start with his social life. Remember that fire and air are two energies that help establish us as independent, autonomous individuals. Anyone with a preponderance of those two elements must work harder to form lasting bonds with people.

From his earliest childhood days, Nash had a reputation for eccentricity. At a high school dance he dragged a pile of stacked-up chairs into the center of the dance floor and started dancing with it. Throughout his childhood Nash never made one close friend. Later, while studying at Princeton, a fellow student recalled his antisocial behavior: "He was always buried in thought. He could easily walk by you and not see you."[2]

What we normally think of as the Venusian and Lunar need for nurturing had been choked off. It's true that both the Moon and Venus are involved in his fire-air complex, but rather than softening these brash energies, the two planets were electrified by them. Friends and colleagues characterized his approach to intimacy as flirtatious and experimental (the Uranus influence). "There was something that happened between people that he didn't experience," one person said.[3]

We can also see Uranus at work in his academic career, which was punctuated by sudden flashes of insight. Nash astounded colleagues in hallways and at conferences, coming up with outlandish propositions that he would proceed to prove in his inimitable Uranian way. One mathematician (whom I'm sure didn't know astrology) said the effect created by one of his hunches was "like lightning striking."[4]

Nash disdained authority of any kind. He read very little, preferring to "rediscover" three centuries of mathematical discoveries for himself.[5] Typical of soft aspects between fire and air (and particularly those involving personal planets), his mind raced from one association to another. One biographer cited a letter Nash had written juxtaposing lunar eclipses, advertising jingles, and mathematical equations. This is vintage Uranus: the linking up of seemingly unrelated phenomena in original ways.

All this is well and good, but perhaps it was a little too good. Because Nash had extremely little earth (Jupiter in Taurus, not strongly aspected and not angular) and a sixth-house Saturn that was removed from the main action, he had very little "containing" energy for this fire-air energy system. Like the red shoes, the fire-air planets ran riot in the playground of his psyche. Nash was living in a super-inflated intellectual universe, largely unconnected to the environment and to his own body. It was one devoid of meaningful connections with other people.

Mars, Uranus & Company burned like wildfire through John Nash's psyche. By the time he was in his early thirties, psychosis had set in. Alone in his electrical universe, Nash imagined himself to be, at various times, the Emperor of Antarctica, a Japanese shogun, and an Arab Palestinian refugee. When he checked into McClean Psychiatric Hospital at age thirty, he said he simply couldn't stop the torrent of ideation flooding his brain.

The Astrology of Transformation

It wasn't until he was well into his fifties that Nash found a way to manage his schizophrenia. He accomplished this by reconnecting with his Saturn and "talking back" to the Uranian fantasies that so disrupted his life. He wrestled control from Mars, Uranus & Company by engaging in a simple psychic activity that he likened to effective dieting: choosing to eat certain healthy foods (Cancerian feelings, Saturnian discretion and control) and rejecting others (the more extreme ideations of Mars-Uranus). The ability to "rationalize" his thinking, he said, was the key factor in his recovery.[6]

This calls to mind the yogic process of witnessing: the practice of taking a couple steps back from whatever we are experiencing and viewing it from afar. In this way, we are able to control, as opposed to *be* controlled, by our emotional reactions.

Framed differently, Nash was employing a Jungian technique called Active Imagination: a process whereby various voices of the psyche are personified and then engaged as if they were separate entities—a therapeutic method we'll see again in the section on Henry Miller in chapter 10. It's a very simple but powerful thing, this "dialoguing" with our inner voices.

Thus, the once dominant players of Nash's psyche, Mars and Uranus, were asked to accommodate to the other voices, particularly his Cancer Ascendant and retrograde Saturn. They were not asked to exit the scene completely, mind you, but to make room for the other members of the team.

"You can only understand the Nash equilibrium if you have met Nash. It's a game and it's played alone."[7] This was said condescendingly by a rival who was trying to prevent the West Virginia mathematician from winning the Nobel Prize. However, I offer it up as a model of mental health: the "game" each of us must play on the road to psychic wholeness.

Astrology teaches us that there are many voices in the psyche—the aggression of Mars, the mothering impulse of the Moon, and the Uranian urge for individuation and uniqueness, to name a few. It is our job is to find a way for all ten to work together as a team. John Nash's life provides a cautionary tale of what can happen when we abandon our role as team "captain" and allow one or two voices to predominate. As Carl Jung once pointed out, the gods are present whether or not they are summoned, and those exiled voices will eventually come back to haunt us. In his struggle with schizophrenia, Nash has given us a powerful model of how to blend even the most dissonant of voices into a symphonic whole.

1. Sylvia Nasar, *A Beautiful Mind* (New York: Touchstone, 1998).

2. Ibid., p. 69.

3. Ibid., p. 181.

4. Ibid., p. 158.

5. Ibid., p. 69.

6. Ibid., p. 354.

7. Ibid., p. 115.

CHAPTER SIX

The Fire Grand Trine

A grand trine occurs when three or more planets are linked in a triangular flow of 120° aspects. Because trines, strictly defined, connect the same elements, the grand trine represents a powerful swirl of elemental energy. When the configuration falls in water, emotion is signified; when the planets are in earth, material security is keyed. In air, intellectual activities are highlighted, and in fire, energy, passion, and self-promotion.

Positive expressions of the grand trine include optimism, resilience, and self-confidence. The grand trine gives the native tremendous reserves of energy and resourcefulness. However, like everything else in astrology, there is a shadow side. Because the energy is so strong (stronger than in either trines or sextiles), exuberance can give way to hubris.

In this and the next three chapters, we'll look at four people with grand trines. We'll see how the grand trine led to inflation and how each person learned to deal (or not deal) with the enormous energy endowed by this configuration.

Marlon Brando

When Marlon Brando died in 2004, the tributes started flowing. "Simply put, in film acting, there is before Brando, and there is after Brando," said the *New York Times*. Jack Nicholson called him a genius who was "the beginning and end of his own revolution."[1]

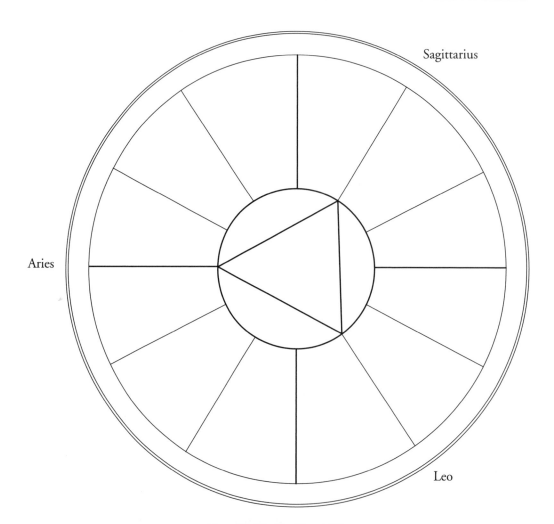

Chart 23: The Fire Grand Trine

For all this, Brando's legacy is built on a handful of brilliant roles—several at the beginning of his career (*A Streetcar Named Desire*, *On the Waterfront*, *The Wild One*), and two extraordinary performances toward the end (*Last Tango in Paris*, *The Godfather*). Most critics agree that he never fulfilled the promise of his early films.

Like many a genius, Brando had a difficult childhood. He was the son of two alcoholics: his father was belittling and abusive and his mother apt to disappear for weeks at a stretch. Brando later recounted tales of how he scoured the bars and honky-tonks of Libertyville, Illinois, in search of his wayward mother. "When you are a child who is unwanted or unwelcome, and the essence of what you are seems to be unacceptable, you look for an identity that will be acceptable," he said. "I suppose the story of my life is a search for love."[2]

We all have our own ways of searching for love, but Brando's was more circuitous than most. He was not liked by the Hollywood establishment, or indeed by many other actors. He had a reputation for being moody and difficult, and for holding up production. It often seemed he went out of his way to make people dislike him. Let's see how his powerful grand trine fed his enormous talent but also contributed to the hubris that derailed his career.

Grand Trine in Fire: Sun-Moon in Aries, Jupiter in Sagittarius, Neptune in Leo

No single aspect can be considered in isolation. Every element of a horoscope must be seen in relation to the whole. This is particularly true for the chart of Marlon Brando, where three powerful configurations—a grand trine in fire, a cardinal t-square, and a mystical yod—all vie for attention (chart 24). We'll examine the yod in chapter 10 and look at the dynamic interplay between Brando's t-square and grand trine in this section.

Brando's grand trine includes an intense Sun-Moon conjunction in Aries, an empowered Jupiter (in its own sign and ruling the Ascendant), and an elevated Neptune in Leo.

Any time you put the Sun and Moon in the same sign, you're going to get a solipsistic orientation to life. The Sun and Moon are the two poles of consciousness, the yin and yang of being. They are usually found in different signs, an important factor in helping people see beyond themselves. For example, if the Sun is in Cancer and the Moon is in Sagittarius, the Cancerian individual then has another way of experiencing the world.

With both lights in the same sign, we have a much tougher time imagining where the other guy is coming from. It helps if Venus, Mars, and Mercury are in other signs. But even so, with the Sun and Moon in the same sign, a great deal of experience is filtered through the prism of the sign they share. The ability to "walk around in the other guy's shoes" becomes all

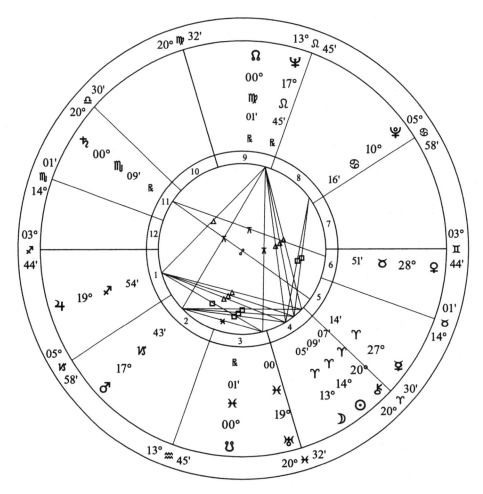

Chart 24: Marlon Brando
April 3, 1924 / 11:00 p.m. CST
Omaha, Nebraska / Placidus houses

the more difficult. Such people simply don't have as much psychic equipment for making the imaginal shift from self to other.

In Brando's Sun-Moon conjunction we find a turbo engine of self-centered, self-involved energy. The Aries energy is boosted by a first-house Jupiter in Sagittarius. This is like the bad boy of the playground (Sun-Moon in Aries) having a buddy on the sidelines (Jupiter in Sagittarius), egging on all his worst impulses.

We find a softening agent in the form of Brando's ninth-house Neptune, as well as a link to his acting prowess. Neptune, the mystic and channeler, helped him tune in to people and then re-create them on stage. When he first met director Elia Kazan on the set of *On the Waterfront*, Brando psyched him out by aping his every move and gesture. The Leo energy enabled the actor to dramatize his Neptunian intuitions.

In Brando's grand trine we see a fiery incarnateness: ego with a capital *E*. "It's like he's carrying his own spotlight," Kazan said.[3] The first time he walked into Stella Adler's famed acting class—in tight blue jeans and a sweaty t-shirt—Adler asked who the vagabond was. "Marlon Brando," said the guy with Sun-Moon conjunct in Aries, and proceeded to stare her down until she blushed. This was a twenty-two-year-old nobody walking into the most respected acting studio of the day. But no matter. Brando was Brando, a revolution unto himself, unfazed by authority figures and icons alike. This is the same cocky intensity moviegoers saw in Stanley Kowalski as he burned holes into Blanche DuBois and destroyed her illusions, the same totalitarian confidence that the actor embodied in *The Godfather*. Whether Marlon, Stanley, or Vito, the fire of Brando's grand trine blazed bright, leaving a trail of ash in its wake.

We've seen how the grand trine powered Brando's immense acting talent. Let's turn now to the primary focus of this section: how soft aspects in general and grand trines in particular can lead to hubris and living beyond our means.

In the beginning, the inflationary energy of Brando's grand trine manifested in a mostly benign way. When Marlon was small, his mother had to take him to kindergarten on a leash—the three planets of his grand trine were not at all happy about the thought of being cooped up in a classroom. His school years were characterized by pranks and rebellion. He was expelled from high school after he poured hydrosulfate into a blower, an act that suffused the building with the odor of rotten eggs. Brando couldn't help himself, one person said of the young Brando's mischief making. With a rampaging grand trine in fire, we can understand why.

As he grew older, his pranks took on a darker cast. By the time he'd achieved fame in *Streetcar*, Brando had taken to driving down Hollywood Boulevard with a fake arrow through his head. "Ha, ha!" you say. But the Hollywood establishment was not amused. Nor were studio heads happy about his refusal to toe the line in interviews and say the things he was supposed to say. Brando, according to one Hollywood insider, was "a time bomb waiting to explode."[4]

It's here we begin to see the rebellion and anger of the t-square mingling with the run-away energy of the grand trine. Let's take a moment to examine the t-square before considering the synergy of the two configurations combined.

The Cardinal T-Square: Sun-Moon in Aries Square Mars in Capricorn and Pluto in Cancer

Sun-Moon in Aries, that powerhouse of self-infatuation, is at the focal point of this cardinal t-square, with Pluto in Cancer on one side and Mars in Capricorn on the other. Is it any wonder that Brando had so many problems with his father? Here are four of the primary power players of the zodiac—Mars, Aries, Pluto, and Capricorn (as well as the main "father" figures)—all in a highly stressful configuration.

Marlon Brando Sr. embodied all the darkest manifestations of power. In addition to being an alcoholic, he was a serial adulterer. He once came home with lipstick smeared on his underwear, which drove his wife into a weeks-long drinking binge. Marlon Jr. said that his father never gave him a word of encouragement.

As the younger Brando aged, we see how the rage of his t-square infected the unbridled energies of his grand trine. Marlon did anything he could to buck the establishment (i.e., his father), throwing temper tantrums during rehearsals and storming out in the middle of scenes.[5]

By the late 1970s, Brando was virtually unemployable—his reputation for being un-cooperative scared most directors from hiring him. Comics started caricaturing the grossly overweight actor on late-night talk shows.

Yet another aspect of the inflationary grand trine was Brando's disastrous purchase of Tetiaroa, an atoll in French Polynesia. Brando hatched grandiose plans for a hotel resort complex, a think tank, and an artist's colony. None of these materialized, due to "inattention" and "unreal expectations."[6]

Although Brando had transformed the art of screen acting, his obstinacy and eccentricity "prevented him from fully realizing the promise of his early genius"—a tragic expression of the shadow sides of both his t-square and grand trine.[7]

The Astrology of Transformation

The morning after Brando died, I had a conversation about the film star with a colleague. "He coulda been a contenda," my colleague said, parroting the line Brando had made famous. My coworker was alluding to all the duds the actor had been in.

There was a moment of silence, after which I said, "He *was* a contender!" Indeed, Marlon Brando won two Oscars and acted in six immortal films. He is widely acknowledged as having revolutionized film acting in the twentieth century.

Our differing perspectives on the enigmatic Brando spoke to the heart of the paradox of his chart. After a burst of creative fire at the beginning of his career, Brando's talent would lie fallow for many years. Could he have achieved more? Undoubtedly yes. But it was remarkable what Brando *did* achieve. At age twenty-three, he had accomplished more than most actors attain in a lifetime. It was almost as if he had sprung fully formed—like Athena from the head of Zeus—onto the Broadway stage in his stunning Broadway debut as Stanley Kowalski. The explosive energy of his grand trine, the anger of the t-square, and, as we'll soon see, the mystical intuition of a Neptunian yod were all on display during that performance.

"Transformation" is an elusive concept. Profound change takes place on many levels, many of them unseen. Such was the complexity of Brando's chart that the arc of change is less apparent than for most. It might be that it will take many more years, and many more biographical studies, before we fully understand the mystery of Marlon Brando's horoscope.

1. R. Lyman, "Marlon Brando, Oscar-Winning Actor, Is Dead at 80," *New York Times*, July 2, 2004, p. 1.

2. Ibid.

3. Patricia Bosworth, *Marlon Brando* (New York: Viking, 2001).

4. R. Lyman, "Marlon Brando, Oscar-Winning Actor, Is Dead at 80."

5. Ibid.

6. Ibid.

7. Ibid.

CHAPTER SEVEN

The Earth Grand Trine

Muhammad Ali

I want everybody to bear witness. I shook up the world! I am the greatest thing that ever lived! I just upset Sonny Liston. . . . I'm the king of the world!
—From *King of the World* by David Remnick[1]

Does the bombast of this quote sound familiar? These words were trumpeted by a precocious twenty-two-year-old named Muhammad Ali after he defeated a famous (and feared) prizefighter named Sonny Liston. We witnessed a similar bravado in the last chapter when Marlon Brando, at the very same age, strutted into Stella Adler's acting class.

Both men had dynamic grand trines in their charts—Brando's was in fire, Ali's in earth. And both were blessed with the Promethean confidence that the grand trine bestows. Both Brando and Ali also had to reckon with the punishment meted out by the gods for the sin of hubris.

Ali's claim to greatness was no idle boast. While still a boy, he informed his parents that he was going to become champion of the world. Later, at a city tournament, the twelve-year-old upstart jumped into the ring and taunted one of the fighters. The organizers of the tournament laughed and shook their heads—"Who *is* this kid?" everyone asked. They

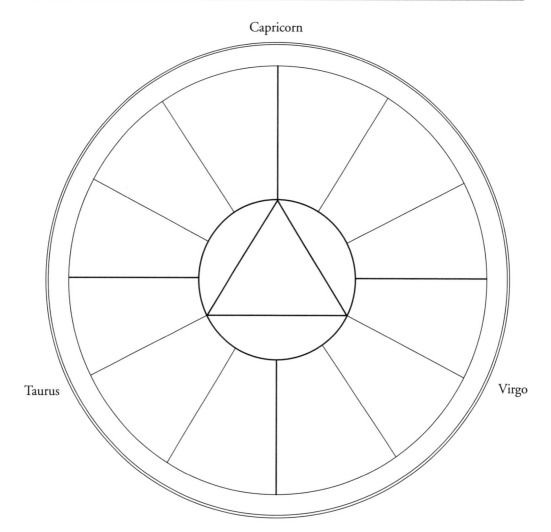

Chart 25: The Earth Grand Trine

didn't have to ask for long. After Ali grabbed the world heavyweight title in 1965, he went on to defeat all the biggest names in boxing.

Even more than athletic prowess, Ali is remembered for his outrageous antics. He shocked onlookers when he seized the mike from a sports commentator at a boxing match. Before his fight with Liston, he stalked the fighter—prancing around on his front lawn and "lunging around like a mental patient."[2] Later, he channeled the immense energy of his grand trine into an impassioned advocacy of black rights. Just as Jackie Robinson broke the color line in baseball, Ali freed black boxers from the death grip of the mob and a cycle of exploitation that left many a black champion penniless.

Ali changed all that. Ali said that he was king of the world, and he was. He also said that he was indestructible. Alas, that was not true. By the time he turned fifty, Ali could barely talk. He even had trouble picking up a phone receiver and cradling it to his ear. The once great boxer had become an old man before his time.

Let's take a look at the dynamic interplay of energies in Ali's chart and how the grand trine powered his career. We'll also see how the overexuberance of that same configuration destroyed his health at a time when he should have been in his prime.

Grand Trine in Earth: Sun in Capricorn, Saturn-Uranus in Taurus, Neptune in Virgo

When you want to talk about who made me, you talk to me.[3]
I had to prove you could be a new kind of black man.
I had to show that to the world.[4]
—Muhammad Ali

As we know, the grand trine is an indicator of robust confidence. In this configuration, Neptune and Uranus inspire and energize the Sun, while Saturn provides an important stabilizing influence, helping Ali to discipline his considerable energies.

In addition to imbuing confidence and strength, the grand trine also works to promote a fierce personal autonomy, something astrologer Noel Tyl calls a "closed circuit" of self-sufficiency.[5] Because Ali's grand trine was in earth, his need to be self-sufficient took on physical dimensions. It's no accident that Ali was a boxer: his body was his weapon and his passport to power. We see another manifestation of his earthy need for incarnateness

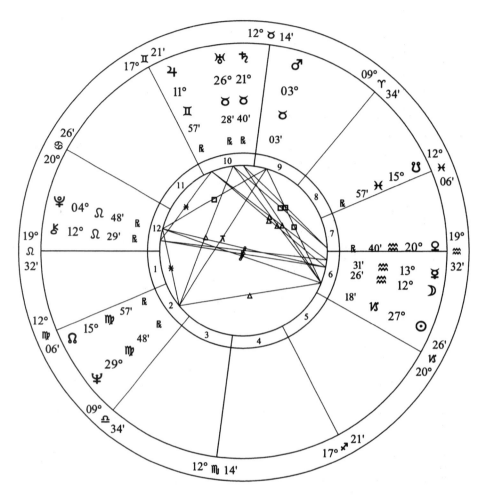

Chart 26: Muhammad Ali
January 17, 1942 / 6:35 p.m. CST
Louisville, Kentucky / Placidus houses

in his desire to own real estate—stocks and bonds just weren't good enough. "There, that's mine," he said. "I want to be able to see it."[7]

There were two things, in addition to his grand trine, that enabled Ali to achieve power and independence: (1) his iron will, courtesy of his Sun-Mars-Pluto t-square, and (2) the help and endorsement he received from the Nation of Islam.

Before Ali arrived on the scene, black fighters had been the unwitting victims of Mafia control and manipulation. Many a black fighter achieved fame only to spend his final days in the poorhouse, robbed of every cent by mob strongmen.

Ali was determined that this would not happen to him. But this presented a problem. Who would underwrite training and living expenses? The Nation of Islam stepped in and filled the void—not only materially but spiritually. In the process, Ali became wholly identified with their ideals.

This might at first appear contradictory. If the grand trine promotes self-sufficiency, why would he become dependent on an organization outside himself? Herein lies the paradox of his chart: While membership in any religious organization, especially one as radical as the Nation of Islam, diminishes one's personal freedom, Ali's association with the Muslims enabled him to achieve financial independence from the mob.

But Ali was not just out for himself. He became an important leader in the civil rights movement of the 1960s. Indeed, Ali played a major role in revamping the image of the African American male in the second half of the twentieth century. An elderly Ali recently stated: "Now you see a commercial on TV. There's three kids—two black, one white. It wasn't like that [when I was a kid]," he said. "Things changed," he said. "And I helped."[8]

The rhetoric of black supremacy espoused by the Muslims allowed Ali to achieve pride as a black man and gave him leverage over the white racist society he despised. The Nation of Islam, and others, told a "narrative of self-sufficiency" that fulfilled the needs of Ali's grand trine to achieve independence and self-respect.[9]

The focus on tribe, on Ali's African roots, is befitting the Aquarian energy in Ali's chart (Moon, Mercury, and Venus in Aquarius, opposing the Ascendant). Aquarius and Uranus have a transpersonalizing effect on anything they touch, something that fueled Ali's deep need to address the concerns of the wider black community.

Ali's independence as a black man was also fueled by his tempestuous Sun-Mars-Pluto t-square. As we saw with Brando, hard aspects between the Sun, Mars, and Pluto indicate conflicts with the father. With Brando, this anger centered on his biological father, eventually spilling over into confrontations with the Hollywood establishment. Ali also had some problems with his father, but the lion's share of rebellion was directed at the white establishment.

An Interplay of Aspects

The main challenge in Ali's chart is that the willfulness of the t-square supercharges the robust energies of the grand trine, pushing him into extreme behaviors that ultimately ruined his health. It's true that his theatrics both inside and outside the ring, as well as his punishing training regimen, paid off handsomely in security and success. But the synergistic exchange between the t-square and grand trine also goaded him into one too many fights. Largely due to his extravagant boasts, Ali was only thirty-nine when he was struck by Parkinson's disease, a nervous disorder that ordinarily doesn't hit until age sixty or later. The disease causes tremors, makes speech difficult, and can freeze the face into a mask. No one knows what causes it, but many researchers believe that accelerated aging is one culprit. Getting hit thousands of times by the strongest men in the world couldn't have helped.

Like many other fighters before him, Ali thought he could emerge intact from years of taking a pounding in the ring. "I won't retire from boxing with cuts, cauliflower ears, and a busted nose," he said. "I'll leave boxing physically intact. I will do this because my style of boxing protects me from cuts and injuries, yet it wins. . . . I cannot be touched!"[10]

However, by his last bout, in 1981, neurological deterioration had already set in, including slurred speech and significantly slowed reflexes. With the inexhaustible confidence of his grand trine, Ali simply couldn't believe that the long years of fighting were taking a toll. "They just won't stop!" said one observer of professional boxers. "So their end is tragic."[11]

The Astrology of Transformation

Here we see why it's the so-called soft aspects that pose the biggest challenges in our charts. Hard aspects push us into highly uncomfortable places. As a result, we do something—anything—to get out. To be sure, sometimes what we do is not the best thing, and that can land us in even more trouble. But in the process there is movement and growth and, hopefully, learning.

Soft aspects, on the other hand, induce complacency. In the case of grand trines, they can create grandiosity that is downright dangerous. As was the case with Brando, it's difficult not to be seduced by the easy energy and robust confidence of the grand trine. People who fall under its spell simply "can't help themselves," as one friend said of Marlon

Brando's pranks. With astrology, though, one can become aware of the danger of the soft aspects and resist the lure.

1. David Remnick, *King of the World: Muhammad Ali and the Rise of an American Hero* (New York: Random House, 1998), p. 200.

2. Ibid., p. 179.

3. Ibid., p. 121.

4. Ibid., p. iii.

5. Noel Tyl, *Synthesis & Counseling in Astrology* (St. Paul, MN: Llewellyn, 1994), p. 285.

6. Remnick, *King of the World*, p. 110.

7. Ibid., p. 305.

8. Ibid., p. 134.

9. Ibid.

10. Ibid., pp. 300–302.

CHAPTER EIGHT

The Air Grand Trine

Lance Armstrong

Here are the characteristics of Virgo, the sixth sign of the zodiac: methodical, hardworking, precise. Ruled by Mercury, Virgos are keenly discriminating and attuned to detail. One of three earth signs, Virgos are also careful and cautious.

Lance Armstrong, champion cyclist, cancer survivor, and seven-time winner of the Tour de France, is a Virgo right down to his racing spats (chart 28). This man has not only Sun in Virgo but Moon, Mercury, and Pluto as well. Although his birth time is not known, I conjecture that he was born in mid to late afternoon, which would place Capricorn on the Ascendant—another earth sign that reinforces the chthonic nature of Virgo.

Now here are the characteristics of Lance Armstrong, at least during the first twenty-five years of his life: tough, pugnacious, reckless. Lance played catch with fireballs as a kid, picked fights with truckers in his teens, and insulted champion European cyclists at international races.

What's happening here? Is this guy really a triple Virgo? Could any of the aforementioned examples be considered careful or cautious behavior?

What's happening is that although Lance has four planets in Virgo, he also has an accentuated Mars in freedom-loving, rule-breaking Aquarius. Lance's Mars is part of a grand trine in air—one of the engines that powered the whirlwind of activity in Armstrong's youth.

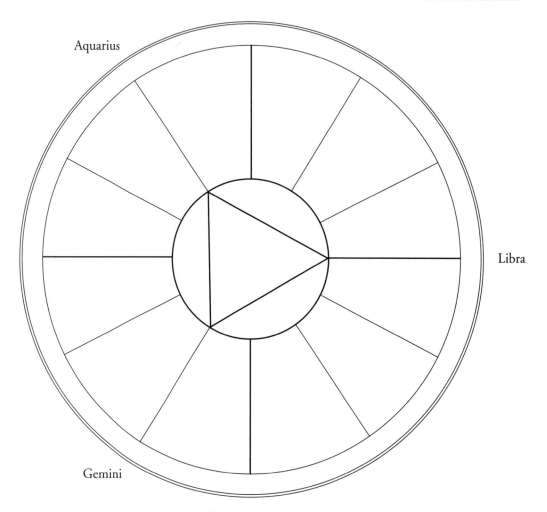

Chart 27: The Air Grand Trine

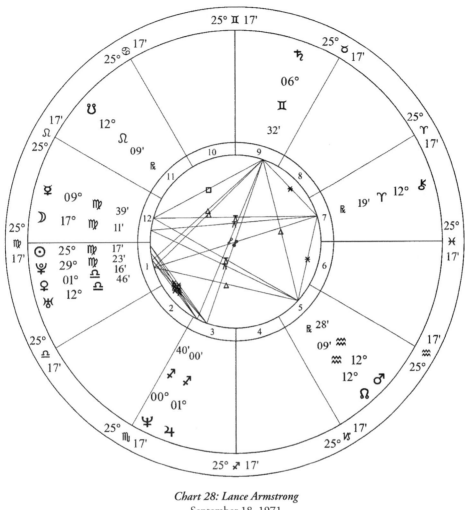

Chart 28: Lance Armstrong
September 18, 1971
Plano, Texas / Sunrise chart

Grand Trine in Air: Mars in Aquarius, Saturn in Gemini, Uranus in Libra

Fueled by his Mars, the grand trine creates a strong urge for independence and freedom. So powerful is this configuration that it nearly eclipsed the considerable Virgo energies in his early years, making the cyclist look and sound more like a fire-breathing Aries than a sign ruled by a virgin. It wasn't until Lance was diagnosed with testicular cancer at age twenty-five that he started to change. His prognosis, which was more like a death sentence with the odds the doctors gave him, put him in touch with the abundant Virgo energies in his chart by braking the Mars-driven whirlwind of his early years. It was this process that enabled him to win the Tour de France, a 2,000-mile bike race that's considered one of the toughest in the world. Lance himself has acknowledged that had it not been for the lessons he learned through his battle with cancer, he never could have won.[1]

How was Lance able to tame the formidable energies of his grand trine? As we saw in the chapter on oppositions, his fight with cancer was one significant factor. Let's take a look at how Armstrong's struggle with life-threatening illness shifted the balance of power in his chart and took the Mars-led grand trine off center stage.

The Astrology of Transformation: Armstrong's Spiritual Awakening and the Resurgence of Virgo

As we have already seen, Lance was the son of a working-class single mom. As an adolescent, he had to contend with an abusive stepfather and a high school where he clearly didn't fit in. Is it any wonder that his Aquarian Mars and grand trine came to play such an overbearing role in his life? That grand trine was not only a way of asserting his masculinity, but it was also an escape from a seemingly no-exit situation.

Lance Armstrong's restless Mars got a big boost when a neighborhood retailer gave his mom a good deal on his first bike—the perfect vehicle for expressing the air sign quest for freedom and mobility.

Despite Lance's initial success on the racetrack, he was in for a rude shock with his diagnosis of cancer. The hopelessness engendered by cancer stops us in our tracks. When we don't have any illusions to fall back on, we slow down and start looking within. Religious devotees undertake this process of their own free will; life-threatening illness imposes it from without.

Lance had been brought to a place of stillness and was about to become acquainted with the bounty of his Virgoan nature. Before he was ready, though, he first needed to become better acquainted with his Mars.

"Better acquainted?" you say. "It looks like he was acquainted enough!"

Well, yes and no. Despite the prominent role that Mars played in his life (evidenced by the fireball games and scrapes of his youth), he couldn't see how destructive the intense energy of the Mars-driven grand trine had become. He needed an outer stimulus to see the imbalanced way in which he was living.

He had his chance when he was introduced to a young oncologist in the early stages of his illness. The man was well-groomed and had the muscular physique of a runner—the very image of the fiercely competitive athlete Lance had been. The doctor began to outline a treatment protocol.

"You will crawl out of here," the doctor informed him. "I'm going to kill you, and then I'm going to bring you back to life. We're going to hit you with chemo, and then hit you again. You're not going to be able to walk."

After the treatment, Lance would be infertile. The treatment would destroy his lungs and prevent him from riding again. "The more he talked," Lance said, "the more I recoiled at the vivid images of my enfeeblement."[2]

If this isn't the voice of an unmodulated Mars, I don't know what is: force for its own sake and to hell with the consequences.

For all the trauma of that meeting, though, there was something extremely important taking place. Lance was getting his own unbridled Mars thrown right back in his face. And he knew it.

Now that Lance had a perspective on the killing power of an unbridled Mars, one amplified by its placement in his grand trine, he slowly started to tap his Virgo energies.

This marked a major change in his life. The Virgo energy in his chart is indispensable to the "gear-combination mathematics" of professional racing and a far cry from the blind desire of an untrammeled Mars![3] By the time he was deemed to be in remission, Lance was harnessing his Virgo planets to win: making a comeback in the circuit of one-day races and preparing to tackle the formidable Tour de France.

The challenge for Lance was *not* to go with the easy energy of his grand trine but to hunker down and honor his Virgo side. The grand trine did not disappear. But whereas it had once hogged the spotlight, it now plays a powerful supporting role to the needs of Armstrong's Sun-Moon-Pluto conjunction in Virgo.

The United States of America

Since the terrorist attacks of September 11, 2001, and particularly throughout the Bush Administration, America's place in the world has undergone a radical overhaul. Two weeks after 9/11, Ira Glass, a popular host for National Public Radio, exclaimed: "Why does the world hate our guts?"[4]

Indeed, the animosity that erupted in the wake of the attacks was truly stunning. From demonstrations in Indonesia to images of Palestinians dancing in the streets, the intense hatred directed at the U.S. was something that most Americans could not comprehend.

The hostility has come not only from Muslim countries. Consider the comments of former Conservative Party member Matthew Parris in Britain. Upon hearing of the collapse of the Twin Towers, Parris blithely remarked: "The bigger they come, the harder they fall."[5]

Or the comments of Dario Fo, an Italian playwright who won the Nobel Prize for Literature in 1997. "The great speculators wallow in an economy that every year kills tens of millions of people with poverty—so what is it to them that 20,000 are dead in New York? . . . this violence is the legitimate daughter of the culture of violence, hunger, and inhumane exploitation."[6]

Why does the world hate the United States so much? What would account for the venom and hyperbole of these criticisms? Surely Fo understands that a handful of speculators on Wall Street does not equal the 280 million people of the United States. And while American culture has its violent aspects, does he really mean to say that all Americans contribute to the "culture of violence, hunger and inhumane exploitation"?

One explanation is America's grand trine in air, a configuration that promotes intellectual hubris and effectively locks others out of its swirl of self-importance.

An Overview of the Natal Chart of the United States

In the natal chart for the U.S., July 4, 1776, at 3:10 a.m., the Sun is at 12° of Cancer. A water sign ruled by the Moon, Cancer is known for empathy and nurturing. The Cancer energy is particularly strong because Venus, Jupiter, and Mercury all inhabit the sign of the crab.

America's desire to be seen as a nurturer and caretaker, or as some would put it, the "world's policeman," is well-known. From the 1947 Marshall Plan, which helped rebuild a devastated Europe after World War II, to peace initiatives and accords in Ireland and the Middle East, the U.S. is clearly a country that looks beyond its borders.

But it is precisely around these issues that we run into problems. Where does nurturing end and imperial overreach begin? America's adversaries argue that the U.S. is more interested in exploiting other countries than in being truly helpful.

One big contributing factor to this perception is the U.S. Moon in Aquarius.

Here we have fixed air and, in contrast to the empathy of Cancer, intellectualism and detachment. It's true that there is a humanitarian urge to the Aquarian Moon, but it is much

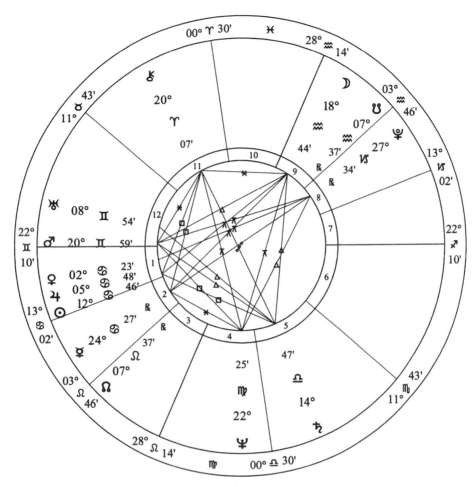

Chart 29: USA, Gemini Ascendant
July 4, 1776 / 3:10 a.m. LMT
Philadelphia, Pennsylvania / Placidus houses

more abstract than America's watery Sun. And because Aquarius is a fixed sign, there is a crusading quality that can incline it toward proselytizing and imposing its values on others.

Tommy Koh, a former Singaporean ambassador to the U.S., wrote a perceptive essay
about America several weeks before the 9/11 attacks that speaks directly to issues relating to the Aquarian Moon. "In the Cold War," Koh said, "the Soviet Union was the most
ideological country in the world. With the end of the Cold War, the U.S. has succeeded
the Soviet Union as the most ideological country in the world. It has elevated democracy,

human rights, and capitalism to the status of dogmas, and any deviation is condemned. The U.S. Mindset is very ideological."[7]

Let's now examine how this very "ideological" Moon behaves within the matrix of America's grand trine in air.

The U.S. Grand Trine in Air: Moon in Aquarius, Mars in Gemini, Saturn in Libra

As we know, grand trines indicate a need for independence as well as present the potential for hubris. When the configuration is in air, a wellspring of intellectual self-sufficiency is indicated. In the U.S. chart, we see Moon in Aquarius trine Mars in Gemini and Saturn in Libra. The U.S. grand trine functions in two ways: (1) to bolster and amplify the Aquarian Moon's drive for human rights and individual freedoms, and (2) to effectively rule out the possibility of other countries dialoguing with us on these points. "What need is there of dialogue?" asks the grand trine in air. "We have the whole thing figured out already. We already have all the answers. There's nothing more to discuss."

Unfortunately, this intellectual inflation is not something most people in the U.S. government and diplomatic corps are aware of. If asked, most Americans would say their country by its nature is open to new ideas and receptive to people and trends from different cultures. On many levels this is true, and it is certainly indicated by Mars in Gemini.

However, in our myriad efforts to play world caretaker/policeman, there has been precious little consideration for value systems other than our own. The most recent examples of this include the U.S. refusal to abide by the decisions of the Kyoto Protocol, as well as the Bush Administration's unilateralism vis-à-vis Iraq. In another context, the members of various antiglobalization movements rightly cite America's prominent role in forcing an industrial culture on Third World and developing nations.

This lack of internationalism is not how most Americans view themselves. As the *New York Times* put it, there is a "broad chasm between the way Americans see themselves and the way they are seen."[8] In this lack of awareness, we have the textbook definition of what Carl Jung called the Shadow: an element of psyche that "contradicts who we would like to see ourselves as, how we would like to be seen in the eyes of others."[9]

For this reason, the shadow often falls into the unconscious and may even be actively suppressed. Thus, we see American's collective inability to see past the best intentions of the Cancer Sun and the humanitarian impulses of the Aquarian Moon.

When this happens, the rest of the world responds with understandable anger. Alluding to the shadow aspects of the American psyche, John Brandon, a Southeast Asia specialist, notes: "The knowledge of most Americans about the rest of the world is still woefully inadequate. The U.S. presence is strongly felt—politically, economically, culturally and militarily—in all corners of the globe. Yet Americans treat their preeminence with indifference, exhibiting little interest in foreign affairs, much as they did before the bombing of Pearl Harbor. The rest of the world senses U.S. indifference, construes it as arrogance, and resents it greatly."[10]

It is the resentment of people locked out of America's grand trine in air.

The Astrology of Transformation

Is there any hope in this discouraging picture? Indeed there is, and we see it all around us, every day. We see it when ordinary citizens contact local mosques and Islamic groups to arrange community meetings and conflict resolution session. We see it in the books that have topped bestseller lists over the past years: books on Islam, on the culture and history of the Middle East, on Osama bin Laden and the roots of terrorism. These are all examples of the grand trine in air seeking to extend itself.

It is an axiom of many religious and depth psychological traditions that the solution to our problems lie within the very things that most disturb and upset us. If the grand trine is part of what got us into this fix (with the stubborn, crusading Aquarian Moon its lead batter), then it just might be the grand trine that gets us out. The Gemini Mars's drive for diversity and Saturn in Libra's love for harmony and democracy can greatly boost this process. The work that remains—and it is considerable—is for us to reacquaint ourselves with the deeper, truer impulses of Sun-Venus-Jupiter in Cancer. Only then can we discover a way to truly look beyond our borders and work toward a greater goal: not merely the economic prosperity of our nation but the welfare of Mother Earth.

---

1. Lance Armstrong, with Sally Jenkins, *It's Not About the Bike* (New York: Berkley Books, 2000).

2. Ibid., p. 99.

3. Claire Martin, "Cycling Becomes Metaphor for Cancer Battle," *Denver Post*, June 4, 2000.

4. NPR report, November 2, 2001.

5. S. Erlanger, "In Europe, Some Scold 'World's Policeman,'" op-ed page, *New York Times*, September 26, 2001.

6. Ibid.

7. T. Koh, "The Ignorance on Both Sides Can Cause Trouble," *International Herald Tribune*, July 26, 2001, p. 4.

8. E. Sciolino, "Who Hates Us? Who Loves Us?" op-ed page, *New York Times*, September 23, 2001.

9. J. Brandon, "Americans Must Correct Their Ignorance of Asia," op-ed page, *International Herald Tribune*, October 23, 2001.

10. Ibid.

CHAPTER NINE

The Water Grand Trine

Kurt Cobain

Consider the function of water in human life: unborn babies float in it, continents are anchored in it, civilizations flourish around it, and crops are nourished and sustained by it.

Water is emotion; it is connection. Without water, there is no life.

Consider, now, the lack of water in the lives of the Generation Xers. A Rutgers University sociologist cites the fact that the United States has the lowest percentage among Western nations of children who grow up with both biological parents. "The United States has the weakest families in the Western world because we have the highest divorce rate and the highest rate of solo parenting," says David Popenoe.[1]

Kurt Cobain, the grunge-rock icon who killed himself at age twenty-seven, grew up during a peak period for divorce. When he was eight, his parents divorced, an event from which he said he never recovered. After the breakup he was shuttled between relatives, at one point living under a bridge. He eventually dropped out of school and started experimenting with heroin and other drugs.

At first glance you might be surprised to learn that his chart—like the human body—is 90 percent water: eight of out ten planets (nine, counting Chiron) are in water signs, including all

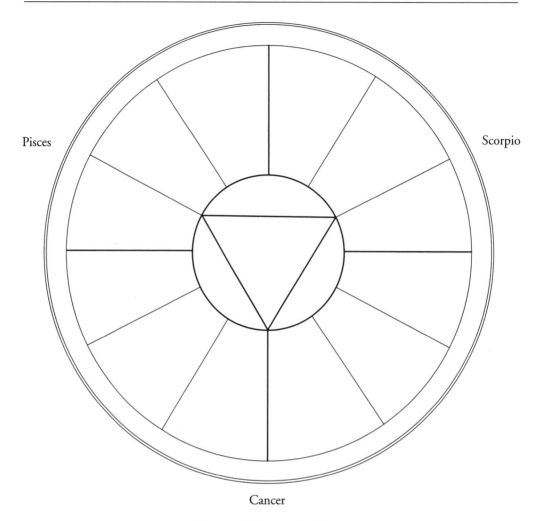

Pisces   Scorpio

Cancer

Chart 30: The Water Grand Trine

five of the personal planets (chart 31). Hearing this, one would think that this tortured soul should have been awash in nurturing and emotion.

He was awash in emotion, all right, but minus the nurturing. For right smack on his Ascendant sits a Uranus-Pluto conjunction—the face of the screeching, screaming grunge performer who mesmerized audiences. Opposing a stellium in Pisces, it is also the seat of much of the angst and upheaval in his chart.

And yet the essence of the chart—Sun, Venus, and Mercury in Pisces, Moon in Cancer—was empathy and sensitivity. "Those who knew the singer," according to a mainstream magazine, "say there was a real fragility buried beneath the noise of his music and his life."[2]

"Hmph," say astrologers. The fragility was not buried at all: it was there and bleeding for everyone to see. What most people—the non-astrologers, that is—saw was the raging Uranus-Pluto conjunction on the Ascendant.

But that was just one aspect of Kurt Cobain. The main problem with this chart is that there is so much water and so much empathy and compassion that Cobain had precious few defenses—against himself and Uranus-Pluto, against his parents, and against the exploitative media that dogged his every move.

Let's look more closely at the grand trine, and how it fed the vulnerability in his chart.

The Grand Trine: Jupiter in Cancer, Neptune in Scorpio, Saturn, Venus, Chiron, and Mercury in Pisces

Before we begin, it's important to take note of the stage on which this grand trine was played out: the Sun is in Pisces and the Moon is in Cancer. Neither are involved in the grand trine, and yet both are in water signs. One of them, the Moon, is in its own sign and extremely potent. Mars in Scorpio, another water sign, is in an exact trine to the Sun. Thus, before we get to the grand trine, we already know that there is too much water and too much easy trine energy for this person's good. What we have, in short, is a recipe for inflation. The grand trine added to an already emotionally indulgent picture.

Jupiter is exalted in Cancer. Jupiter is the largest planet in our solar system. It's the planet of grace, energy, and optimism. In charts of great tension, we turn to Jupiter for a ray of hope. However, here it worked to Cobain's detriment. Because it is exalted, it inflated the already grandiose emotional Cancerian energy and aggravated the other legs of

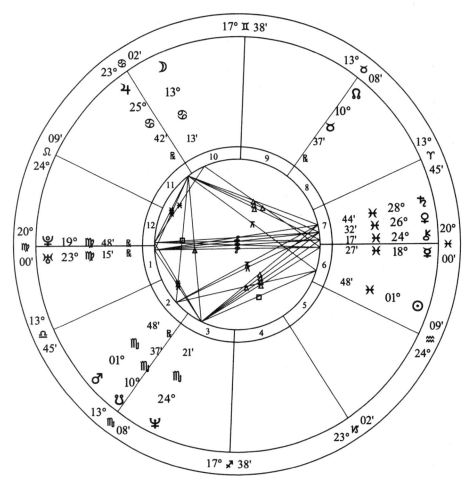

Chart 31: Kurt Cobain
February 20, 1967 / 7:20 p.m. PST
Aberdeen, Washington / Placidus houses

the grand trine. One of those legs, Venus in Pisces, is another exalted planet. Compassion-ate and idealistic, Venus reinforces Cobain's watery Sun and Moon.

But beware: when Venus in Pisces' need for nurturing is not met, when the deep em-pathy and idealism of this placement are not echoed in the other, there can be resentment and self-pity. This planetary picture is immensely complicated by the fact that Venus is conjunct both Saturn and Chiron, two of the most painful places in a horoscope.

To understand the implications this had for Cobain's life, let's take a moment to consider solar arcs and their significance for Cobain's life.

Solar Arcs and Psychic Unfoldment

Solar arcs are a method of prediction whose power is predicated on the correspondence between the 360° of the zodiac and the 365 days of the year. Because one degree roughly equals one year, predictions can be made based on when planets and angles hit significant places in the natal chart. For example, Mars at 2° Virgo in the twelfth house will reach the Ascendant, at 20° Virgo, at age eighteen. At that time the astrologer may make predictions about Mars-related energies and activities. If there are corroborating transits or progressions in other areas of the chart, the likelihood of that energy being expressed will be even greater.

Solar arcs symbolize a maturation of planetary energies. In this case, solar arc Mars hitting the Ascendant will signal an awakening of aggressiveness and self-assertion within the native. Solar arcs are a kind of initiation, a coming of age of a particular planetary archetype. If the individual has split off or sidelined that energy from consciousness, the effect will be even more dramatic.

Looking at Cobain's chart, we see the Sun in the sixth house, 19° from the Descendant. It's no mistake that it was at age nineteen that Nirvana, the band that transformed both rock music and Kurt Cobain, was formed. Solar arc Mars hit the IC/MC axis that same year. The effect of both arcs was that the solar energy came bursting across the threshold of consciousness when Cobain turned nineteen. For the singer, it was a dramatic coming of age.

Let's now examine the Pisces planets and what happened when they were activated by solar arc.

Between the ages of seven and nine, solar arc Descendant hit the Venus-Saturn conjunction—first striking Venus, then the Venus/Saturn midpoint, and finally Saturn. As we know, Cobain's parent's divorced when he was eight, an event that scarred him for life.

Tragically, it was this same place—the Venus/Saturn midpoint—that was activated when Cobain committed suicide at age twenty-seven. That year, solar arc Sun hit Venus/Saturn, reigniting the searing pain from his childhood.

In essence, two aspects of Cobain's psyche were "meeting" for the first time: the Sun-Mars trine (the same trine that midwifed the birth of Nirvana) and the painful Venus/Saturn midpoint—doubly charged by its connection to the grand trine and its opposition to the Uranus-Pluto conjunction.

We could take this analysis one step further and view this chart as two grand trines (Jupiter, Neptune, Venus-Saturn and Sun, Moon, and Mars). When solar arc Sun hit Cobain's Venus-Saturn conjunction, these two grand trines met for the first time. It was like two tidal waves crashing together. Given the pain of the Venus-Saturn-Chiron cluster, it proved too much for him.

The Astrology of Transformation

On one level, Kurt Cobain's life was too short for deep and far-reaching transformation to take place. On another, transformation absolutely occurred: the life that might have started and ended with heroin addiction became an incredible odyssey into the world of rock and roll.

Is there a way this chart *might* have worked on a longer-range basis? How could Cobain have mastered the energy of his grand trines?

We'll never know. One thing is clear: at this point in human evolution, we're better at working with hard aspects than with soft ones. We're better at rising to the challenge of hard aspects than bucking the complacency of soft aspects and exalted planets.

Water is all well and good. Exalted and dignified planets are wonderful. Trines are lovely and flowing. And yet all these lovely things combined can produce indulgence and vulnerability that are not easily counterweighted.

---

1. Sharon Jayson, "Divorce Declining, but So Is Marriage," *USATODAY.com*, July 18, 2005, http://www. usatoday.com/news/nation/2005-07-18-cohabit-divorce_x.htm.

2. J. Giles, "The Poet of Alienation," *Newsweek*, April 18, 1994, pp. 33–38.

PART THREE

Other Aspects

CHAPTER TEN

The Inconjunct and the Yod

The Inconjunct

The inconjunct is a 150° aspect that produces vague and yet deep feelings of tension and discontent. The vagueness is the main challenge. Unlike a square or an opposition, where the energies are clearly defined, the planets in an inconjunct manifest in a more subterranean way.

Let's consider a couple of examples. What connection does the earthy fixity of Taurus have with the fiery mutability of Sagittarius? One is sensual, the other experimental and exploratory. Or compare the quicksilver, cerebral quality of Gemini with the depth and compulsion of Scorpio. Again, no relation. Conversely, consider Gemini and Sagittarius—opposing energies—and we see two mutable signs in compatible elements. Or Gemini and Virgo (a square): incompatible elements but two mutable signs.

The inconjunct is like putting a Russian cossack into the same room with a New York socialite. What in the world will they talk about? How will they connect?

With the inconjunct, the native must find if not a connection then at least a workability between these alien energies.

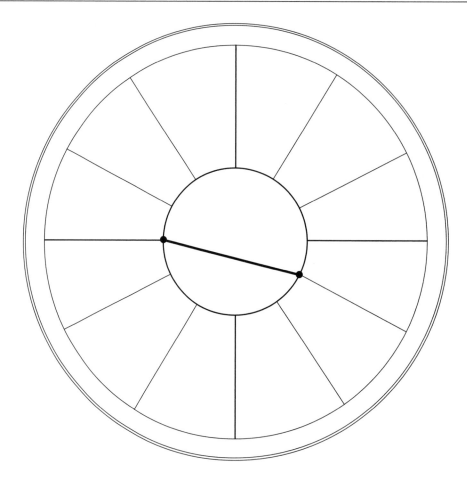

Chart 32: The Inconjunct—150°

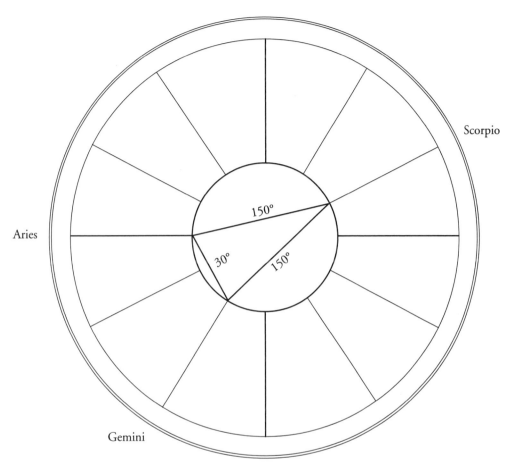

Chart 33: The Yod

The Yod

The yod is a curious and mysterious configuration. Also called the "finger of God," it involves two 150° inconjuncts and a linking sextile at the base. Astrologers disagree as to the ultimate significance of the yod. Unlike other configurations that manifest in dynamic and identifiable ways, the yod is more insidious. While a square can take the form of outer battles and an opposition in contradictory impulses, the yod manifests as inchoate feelings of dis-ease. The native feels pulled in opposing directions, but rarely in ways she can articulate, at least not in the beginning. It can take years to become conscious of the workings of a yod, and longer to gain some control over these energies. In readings, clients will readily identify with descriptions of squares, oppositions, and conjunctions. They will identify much less with descriptions of yods, and this is particularly true for younger clients—the awareness is simply not there yet.

To get a sense of where the yod is trying to go, look to the apex planet: it speaks of the native's destiny or raison d'être. Depending on other factors, the apex planet is the most conscious and easily identifiable energy in a yod.

Henry Miller

Henry Miller, one of the most convention-shattering writers of the twentieth century, has pronounced Scorpionic energies in his chart. This will come as no surprise to anyone who knows of Miller's legendary place in the American literary pantheon. His writing was ribald and inflammatory. No holds were barred when it came to writing about sex, which is about what you'd expect from someone with a Moon-Mars-Uranus conjunction in Scorpio in the seventh house. Miller's books were banned in America until the Supreme Court declared the sale of his first novel, *Tropic of Cancer*, constitutionally protected.

Henry Miller was born with Sun in Capricorn to a working-class German immigrant family in Brooklyn, New York. The dueling protagonists (Capricorn versus Uranus) that powered Millers' psyche took on shadow manifestations in the first half of his life: Capricorn in the form of derisive criticism and condemnation from his mother, and Uranus in chaotic disruptions and scattershot rebellions against authority figures. It would take Miller many years to alchemize these two energies and funnel them into his art. We'll see how the yod created a bridge from the unconscious to the conscious and, in so doing, transformed Miller's destructive impulses into raw materials for his writing.[1]

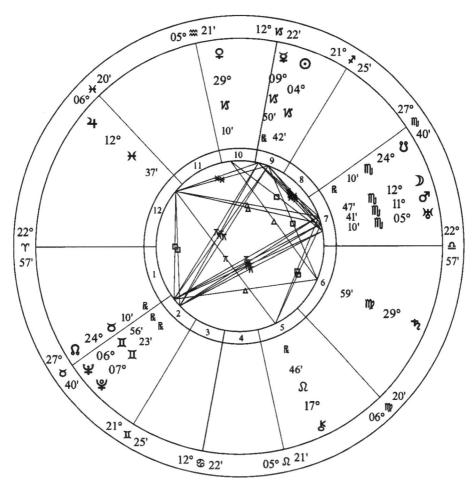

Chart 34: Henry Miller
December 26, 1891 / 12:30 p.m. EST
Manhattan, New York / Placidus houses

The Yod: Neptune-Pluto in Gemini (Apex), Sun in Capricorn, Uranus in Scorpio
Sun in Capricorn Sextile Uranus in Scorpio

In this sextile we'll see how two very different drives—Capricornian order and Uranian chaos—manifested in Miller's life. We can see the ancestral origins of the split between Capricorn-Saturn and Uranus in Miller's family. Although both his parents emigrated from Germany, his father's side were the wild ones: a ragtag collection of Bavarian ship captains, riverboat pilots, and earth wanderers. His mother's family came from Bremen: refined and status-conscious. Henry's mother was convinced she had married beneath her station. She classed Henry in the same category as the raffish relatives from her husband's family. This "Teutonic frigidity" would haunt Miller throughout his life, finding echoes in relationships with critical, condemning women.[2]

Henry oscillated between the extremes of Saturnian order and Uranian chaos. In childhood he played the Capricornian good boy that his mother wanted—a bright student who wrote short stories in his free time. Although he showed promise, there was no higher expectation for him than to succeed his father in the family tailoring business.

The strongly Uranian/Scorpionic strain in his character chafed at this. He'd work a month or two balancing the books and then take off on a weeks-long blitz of the dance halls and whorehouses of lower Manhattan. Throughout his childhood and early adulthood, Henry was a terror for any authority figure who crossed his path. This rebelliousness was Uranus talking: the part of his psyche that refused to conform to anyone else's rules.

As we've seen, when one planetary archetype is strong, it manifests not only as inner compulsions but in the form of apparently unrelated forces from without. Such was the case with Henry and June Mansfield, Miller's wife, love, muse, and tormentor. She was the person who most dramatically enacted the Scorpionic energies in Henry's yod.

June Mansfield: The Wild Side of Miller's Yod

Henry and June first met in the summer of 1923 at a Manhattan dance hall where June worked as a taxi dancer. Henry was thirty-three and writing only sporadically. Of all the complex forces encapsulated in Miller's seventh-house conjunction, the lightning-rod energies of Uranus were the ones most immediately apparent in this mesmerizing woman. June sidled up to him and asked if he wanted to dance. She had a "drugged, sleepy, dreamy animal aura about her," with a touch of the gypsy.[3]

Henry was spellbound from the start. It was only a matter of weeks before he left his wife and daughter and was squandering his money on this otherworldly creature.

We can see the Scorpionic energies of Miller's seventh-house conjunction in his probing dissection of June. He grilled her relentlessly about every dark corner of her life. The only problem with these sessions is that, more often than not, June's stories turned out to be untrue: fictions constructed for Henry's amusement and obfuscation. In the end, he never knew whether June was lying or telling the truth, no matter how earnest her declarations. He ultimately came to doubt not only her reality but his own.

It was as if Henry had been sucked into a vortex. But what was really happening? In meeting June, Henry had entered into a confrontation with the splintered, fragmented personality he had become. It was a personality born not only of the deep split between his Saturn-ruled Sun and the Scorpio-Uranus conjunctions but of the contradictions within the Scorpio configuration. In stunning synchronicity, June Mansfield mirrored back to Henry these inner conflicts.

The challenge for Henry was not only to find a balance between Capricorn and Uranus but to incorporate both into his art. The most important challenge for him was to become aware of the shadow sides of both energies, something that took place through the mediating function of the yod, and particularly through the focalizing energies of Neptune.

The Astrology of Transformation: Neptune-Pluto in Gemini

It was through the mystical energies of a literary Neptune-Pluto conjunction in Gemini, the apex of his yod, that Henry was able to transform the angst of his early years. This happened after June shipped Henry off on a steamship to London, where he disembarked and headed to Paris with only a few dollars in his pockets.

Although Henry had been scribbling for years, this was the real beginning of his career as a writer. It was in Paris that Henry wrote his masterpiece, *Tropic of Cancer*. On the surface, *Tropic of Cancer* tells of Miller's encounters with various people he met during his early years in France. However, ultimately these character studies depicted his own fragmented personality—one torn to shreds by a rampaging Uranus. The theme of his books, as one critic put it, was death and the disintegration of the self. Underlying this was something deeper: the inner life of the artist who can survive anything and yet remain "full of joy."[4] The same fragmented self that June reflected back to him was now redefined in his writing—focalized by the Neptune-Pluto conjunction.

It's as if Neptune-Pluto, the transformational writer, had been sent in as a mediator to settle the intractable dispute between the antithetical energies of Capricorn-Uranus. What had once been rage about his personal humiliation (vis-à-vis his mother and his working-class status in the United States) was transformed into anger at the injustices of U.S. institutions and the values of the American mainstream. It was an anger that infused his writing and that ultimately transformed mainstream sexual mores and presumptions.

Tropic of Cancer is the byproduct of the synthesis of the Capricorn and Uranus energies in his chart. Whereas Capricorn had previously manifested as a hypercritical condemnation and negation, it was now a steely discipline: Miller woke up every morning and wrote at least 5,000 words. Where Moon-Mars-Uranus in Scorpio had once manifested in drunken binges and nights out on the town, it now took on the form of a focused and scathing critique of American society. The yod, through the alchemizing powers of Neptune-Pluto, played a powerful role in this process. Please note, however, that mastering a yod takes time. It wasn't until age forty-three that Miller wrote his masterpiece.

Marlon Brando

The Yod: Neptune in Leo (Apex), Mars in Capricorn, Uranus in Pisces

We return to the chart of Marlon Brando, this time to examine how a yod manifested in his life.

Like Miller, Brando had Neptune at the apex. However, in Brando's chart it is in Leo, and the most elevated planet in the chart. Neptune in Leo is a perfect description of Brando's acting talent. It endowed him with a gift for mystically tuning in to other people and then re-creating them on stage.

We've already seen how this manifested on the set of *On the Waterfront*, where Brando first met director Elia Kazan. Now listen to what Kazan said of Brando's acting talent: "He didn't look at you, and he hardly acknowledged what you were saying. He was tuned into you, without listening to you intellectually or mentally. It was a mysterious process."[5]

Indeed, Neptune is a very mysterious planet. Because it is so prominently placed in Brando's chart, it is very powerful as well.

Another characteristic of Neptune is compassion. Despite Brando's surface pugnacity, he exhibited a deep empathy for the suffering of others.

Brando was acutely aware of people's pain—particularly of those less fortunate than himself. As a child, he once brought home a bag lady and insisted his parents give her shelter. As he matured, the actor took up the cause of Native Americans, participating in marches and making controversial speeches at the Academy Awards. Unfortunately, Brando voiced his support with such venom that he turned off many people who would have ordinarily supported such causes.

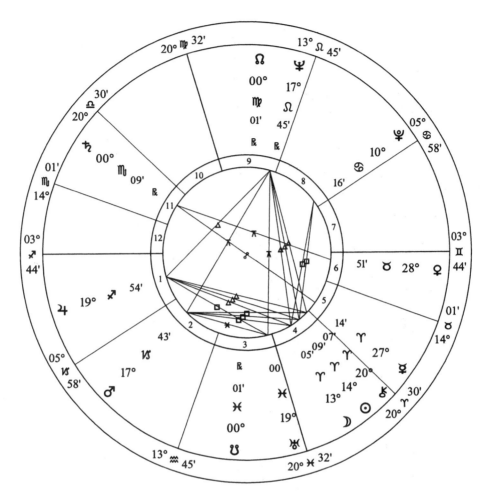

Chart 35: Marlon Brando
April 3, 1924 / 11:00 p.m. CST
Omaha, Nebraska / Placidus houses

It's here that we again see the importance of considering each aspect and configuration in the context of the total chart. For while Brando's Neptune (and ruling Venus in Taurus) wanted to help people who are poor and underprivileged, his combative t-square, and the hubris of the grand trine, all but ensured that he would alienate others in the process. Perhaps this wouldn't have been the case if Brando had been able to alchemize the more challenging energies of his t-square and grand trine. Alas, this was something he was never to achieve. As a result, the actor spent the final years of his life in near isolation. There is greatness in Brando's chart, but ultimately Marlon Brando was more victim than master of his horoscope.

Martha Stewart
The Yod: Moon in Sagittarius (Apex), Mercury in Cancer, Saturn-Uranus in Taurus

We've already seen how Martha Stewart's Sun-Pluto conjunction powered her phenomenal success. We've also witnessed how a dynamic fire-sign trine between Sun and Mars enabled her to function in the fiercely competitive business world.

But why did she choose to build a multimillion-dollar empire around that most feminine of realms, the home? Nothing in her fiery Sun or Mars indicates such an inclination. And yet this is how Stewart describes her life's work: "Making a home, raising a family, was more important to me than anything else. I decided . . . that the home was really my place. I really loved it. I loved the garden. I loved decorating, designing, cooking."[6]

This is baffling until we notice that obscured in the ferment of Stewart's chart is a yod between the Moon, Mercury, and Saturn-Uranus. The Moon, the archetypal symbol of home and nurturing, is at the apex.

Intriguingly, Mercury is in Cancer, the Moon's sign. Thus, there is reception between these two planets. In addition, the inconjunct between Mercury and the Moon is exact, making it all the more potent. Finally, the lunar realm of home is even stronger because of the Moon's "bucket handle" placement in the chart.

As we've seen, the apex planet is the most prominent of the three energies in a yod. Clearly, this has been the case with Stewart. After a brief flirtation as a stockbroker in the early years of her career, she knew she wanted her business empire centered around the home.

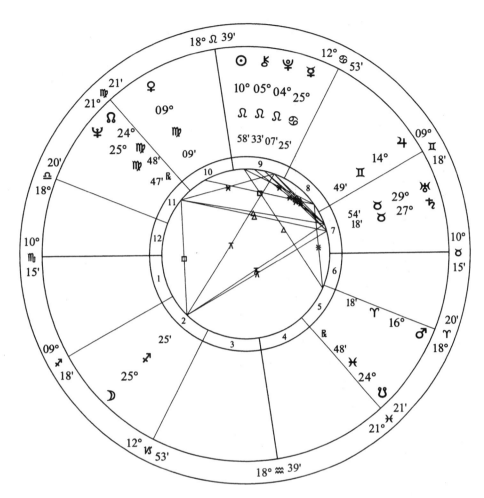

Chart 36: Martha Stewart
August 3, 1941 / 1:33 p.m. EDT
Jersey City, New Jersey / Placidus houses

The home, as symbolized by the apex of her yod, is the perfect theater for the histrionic inclinations of her Leo Sun. It provided the ideal backdrop for her lush coffee-table books as well as her magazine, *Martha Stewart Living*. The Saturn-Uranus leg (in Taurus) completes this picture. The Saturn-Uranus energies are intimately tied up with the father—not only through Saturn but through Uranus's rulership of her fourth house. Indeed, it was Stewart's father who initiated her into the wonders of gardening, sparking a lifelong love. The fact that he was so demanding further fueled the power needs of her Sun and Mars.

1. Jay Martin, *Always Merry and Bright: The Life of Henry Miller* (New York: Penguin, 1978).

2. Ibid., p. 4.

3. Ibid., p. 77.

4. Ibid., p. 305.

5. Patricia Bosworth, *Marlon Brando* (New York: Viking, 2001), p. 47.

6. Virginia Meachum, *Martha Stewart: Successful Businesswoman* (Berkeley Heights, NJ: Enslow Publishers, 1998), p. 27.

CHAPTER ELEVEN

Non-Ptolemaic Aspects

The Semisquare

The semisquare is a 45° aspect that indicates conflict. The tension of the semisquare, however, is not as pronounced as that of the square. The native knows there is a problem but is not quite sure how to handle it. Because the semisquare is only 15° from a sextile, the planets involved are sometimes found in compatible elements, making the energetic interchange even more ambiguous and difficult to define.

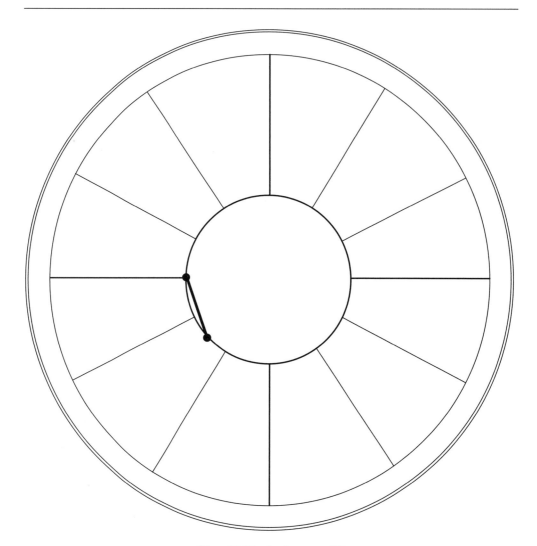

Chart 37: The Semisquare—45°

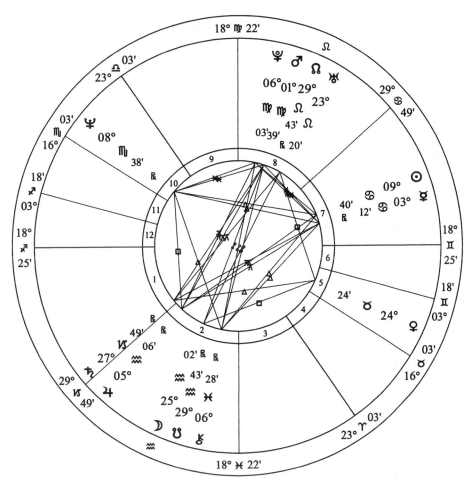

Chart 38: Princess Diana
July 1, 1961 / 7:45 p.m. GMD
Sandringham, England / Placidus houses

Princess Diana: Venus in Taurus Semisquare Sun in Cancer

As we know from earlier chapters, Diana experienced a lifelong struggle between the intimacy needs of her Cancer Sun and the need for detachment suggested by the Venus-Uranus square. We see that Diana also had a semisquare between Venus and the Sun, suggesting yet more tension between these two impulses. Thus, although there is elemental compatibility between earth and water, the particular degrees involved make for an uneasy relationship between the two. We'll see in the section on sesquiquadrates later in this chapter how this situation was aggravated still further.

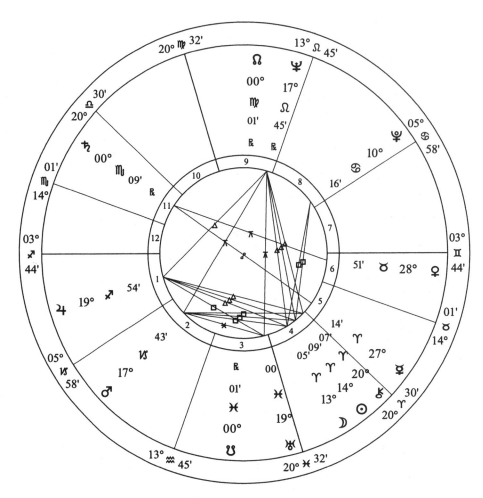

Chart 39: Marlon Brando
April 3, 1924 / 11:00 p.m. CST
Omaha, Nebraska / Placidus houses

Marlon Brando: Venus in Taurus Semisquare Sun-Moon in Aries

We already know of the incredible complexity of this chart from earlier chapters: there's a grand trine in fire, a volcanic t-square involving the Sun, Mars, and Pluto, and a mystical yod with Neptune at the apex.

One of the few planets not involved in this maelstrom is Venus. This is quite interesting, given the fact that Venus is dignified—in its own sign. In addition, it does not make any Ptolemaic aspects to other planets, which gives it great weight in the chart. Imagine how this powerful Venus felt not being part of the main action. One could liken this situation to a kid at a birthday party whom no one talks to. Eventually that kid is going to make a lot of noise to get heard.

However, Venus does form a semisquare to Brando's Sun-Moon conjunction. This suggests an uneasy relationship between the fire of Brando's Sun and Moon and the sensuality and compassion of his ruling Venus. The effect was to give the sympathy of Venus a martial cast. Thus it was that Brando was known to take up causes (preferably lost causes), but with such belligerence that he often turned off the very people he was trying to win over. A case in point was his combative support for Native Americans, an approach that eventually alienated many of the people he was trying to help!

The main problem here is that although Brando identified with the plight of the disenfranchised and sincerely wanted to help, the combined tension of the semisquare and t-square made for a pugnacious advocate. In order to work mindfully with this aspect, Brando would have had to become aware of his behavior and then ask himself if confrontation was really the best way to get the job done.

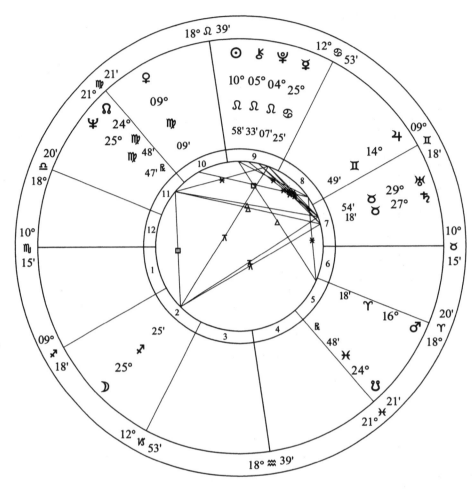

Chart 40: Martha Stewart
August 3, 1941 / 1:33 p.m. EDT
Jersey City, New Jersey / Placidus houses

Martha Stewart: Sun in Leo Semisquare Neptune in Virgo

Martha Stewart is singularly equipped to compete in the cutthroat corporate environment of the American mainstream. With Sun in Leo trine Mars in Aries—two masculine planets, dignified, in two masculine elements—she not only survives but thrives. Her Sagittarian Moon infuses this picture with yet more yang energy.

However, in the semisquare between Leo and Virgo, the power needs of a narcissistic tenth-house Sun clash with both the otherworldliness of Neptune and the humility and self-restraint of Virgo.

Let's look at the challenges posed by Neptune. Clearly, Martha Stewart is not a person we associate with spirituality or transcendence, and yet the semisquare suggests that this will become part of her path. It's still too early to tell, but it might be that the confinement of prison life awakens the Neptunian energy in her chart. The fact that Neptune is in Virgo also suggests that incarceration will teach her humility and self-restraint. Interestingly, transiting Neptune conjuncted her IC in early 2006. In addition, solar arc Jupiter will conjunct the MC in 2007. I predict that Stewart will indeed learn important lessons during her prison term and will emerge stronger and wiser at the end of it.

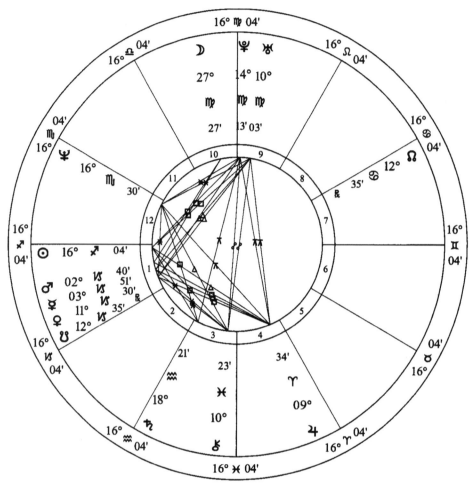

Chart 41: Princess Masako
December 9, 1963
Tokyo, Japan / Sunrise chart

Princess Masako of Japan: Mars-Mercury in Capricorn Semisquare Saturn in Aquarius

Princess Masako must find a way to reconcile two antithetical energies in her chart. On one side we find Sun in Sagittarius and possibly a Sagittarian Ascendant. We also see Jupiter in Aries—more fire. In short, Masako has a deep need for freedom and adventure. The international life she led in the first half of her life, before she married Prince Naruhito, was an expression of those energies.

On the other side is a daunting conjunction between Uranus and Pluto, which squares her freedom-loving Sun. In Uranus-Pluto we see the constrictions of the royal life she's led since her marriage.

The conflict of this square is echoed by a semisquare between Mercury-Mars in Capricorn (the astrological embodiment of the palace bureaucrats who try to control her every move) and Saturn in Aquarius (an echo of the Sagittarian energy in her chart).

There's a good deal of ambiguity in Masako's semisquare. While Aquarius yearns for freedom, Saturn does everything in his power to work against it. There is a similar dynamic in the square: while Pluto and Virgo clearly signal the duty and restriction of palace life, freewheeling Uranus tells a different story. There is a suggestion here that the palace bureaucrats themselves, despite all their words to the contrary, are yearning for a change.

How will Masako reconcile these two sides of her being? How will she satisfy her deep yearning for freedom while not forgetting her duties as a Japanese princess? In essence, what Masako must do is find a way to both revolutionize duty and redefine freedom. Nothing else will satisfy the demands of this chart. If she succeeds, she will become a symbol for millions of women in Japan struggling with similar issues. If she fails, the Sagittarian energies will continue to atrophy as Uranus-Pluto terrorizes in the form of the palace bureaucrats.

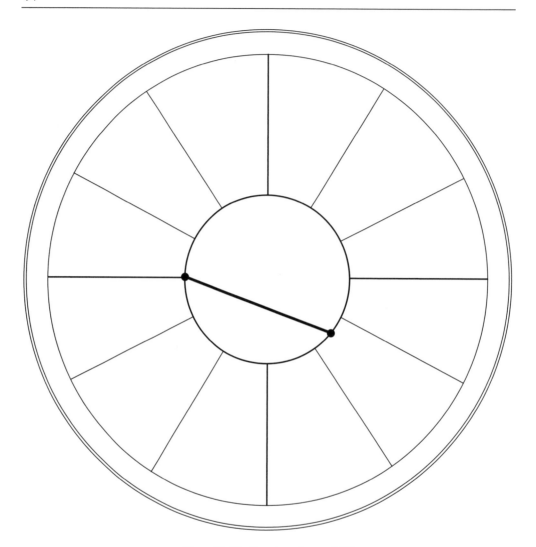

Chart 42: The Sesquiquadrate—135°

The Sesquiquadrate

The sesquiquadrate, a 135° aspect, manifests like a square: two planets in tense relationship representing needs that are not compatible.

However, the sesquiquadrate is a contradictory aspect. Although it indicates conflict, it is only 25° away from being a trine, the softest of the soft aspects. As a result, it often links planets in the same element—something that would ordinarily indicate a harmonious relationship. Because of the angle involved, though, this "trine" has an extra charge. In some ways, the sesquiquadrate can be thought of as a very favorable aspect: it has the underlying compatibility of a trine, but without the complacency. But one must possess sufficient awareness to handle the energies of this aspect in a constructive manner. As we'll see, this is more easily said than done.

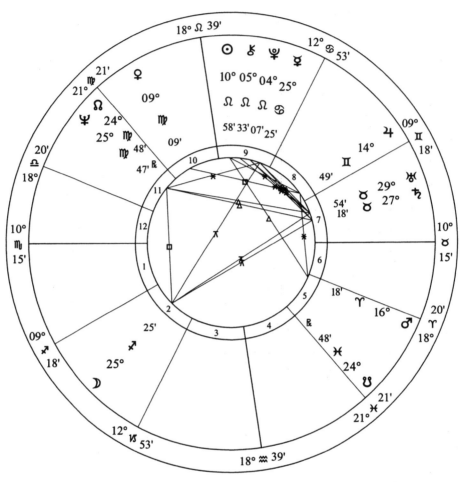

Chart 43: Martha Stewart
August 3, 1941 / 1:33 p.m. EDT
Jersey City, New Jersey / Placidus houses

Martha Stewart: Sun in Leo Sesquiquadrate Moon in Sagittarius

We return for another look at dynamo Martha Stewart. Here we find her Sun and Moon in a tense sesquiquadrate relationship. At first glance it is hard to imagine what the difficulty might be: the adventurous optimism of the Sagittarius Moon appears to blend seamlessly with the creative force of her Leo Sun. Stewart herself has no problem with this combination. She often cites her role as teacher (a classic Sagittarian career) in her desire to revive the domestic arts. The Leo Sun packages these Sagittarian "lessons" with great flair—whether through lavish coffee-table books or dynamic television shows.

However, this is not the view of her detractors. They see not the philosophical expansionism of her Sag Moon but the shadow side of an elevated, ruling Sun: opportunism and self-aggrandizement.

How might Stewart work to resolve this conflict? One approach—putting less emphasis on empire building (the elevated Sun) and more on community outreach (Sagittarius Moon)—might be a way to recalibrate the energies in her chart.

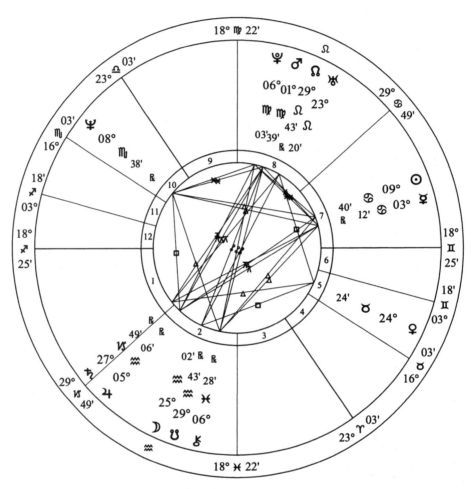

Chart 44: Princess Diana
July 1, 1961 / 7:45 p.m. GMD
Sandringham, England / Placidus houses

Princess Diana: Sun in Cancer Sesquiquadrate Moon in Aquarius

Here we see another Sun-Moon sesquiquadrate, but this time in two incompatible elements: water and air. The elemental conflict is just one of the problems. The ruling planets associated with these signs—Moon and Uranus—are antithetical as well.

Indeed, the disconnect indicated by this sesquiquadrate mirrors the main conflict of Diana's chart: the need for nurturing and connection (Cancer) versus the urge for freedom and detachment (Moon in Aquarius, Sagittarius Ascendant, Venus square Uranus). Diana alchemized this conflict by taking her very personal need for love and "transpersonalizing" it: going out into the world and ministering to the world's forgotten and oppressed—whether they were homeless women in the streets of London or land mine victims in Bosnia.

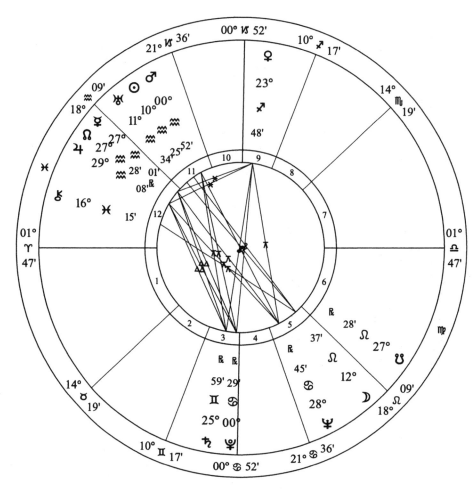

Chart 45: Thomas Merton
January 31, 1915 / 9:00 a.m. GMT
Prads, France / Placidus houses

Thomas Merton: Sun-Uranus in Aquarius Sesquiquadrate Saturn in Gemini

This is the chart of Thomas Merton, a Catholic mystic who entered a Trappist monastery at age twenty-six and spent much of the rest of his life in silent contemplation. His most famous work, an autobiography called *The Seven Storey Mountain*, has been translated into more than twenty languages. It is considered one of the greatest spiritual memoirs ever written.

The first years of Merton's life were marked by tragedy. Born in 1915 to two American expatriates in France, his mother died when Merton was only six and his father when he was sixteen.

Not long after, Merton embarked on a period of dissipation, part of which he chronicles in *The Seven Storey Mountain*. His need for freedom and experimentation is not surprising, with five planets in Aquarius, including a Sun-Uranus conjunction. In addition, Merton had Aries rising and Moon in Leo. He had no earth in his chart.

Most people cannot tolerate a life without structure or rules for long, and this was definitely true for Merton. It was when both transiting Saturn and Uranus were squaring his Aquarius stellium that Merton rejected secular life and entered the monastery.

His rationale for doing so speaks volumes about his conflicted relationship with the Aquarian energy in his chart. "We live in a society whose whole policy is to excite every nerve in the human body and keep it at the highest pitch of artificial tension, to strain every human desire to the limit and to create as many new desires and synthetic passions as possible, in order to cater to them with the products of our factories and printing presses and movie studios and all the rest."[1] Thus it was that Merton rejected the "excitation" of the Uranian energies, choosing instead to retreat to "the four walls of my new freedom"—a remote monastery in the hills of Kentucky.

The sesquiquadrate between his Sun-Uranus conjunction and Saturn in Gemini was the saving grace of this chart, the hinge on which Merton's transformation occurred. Although it connects two air signs (Aquarius and Gemini), the tension between the Saturn and Uranus archetypes predominates. It ultimately forced Merton to commit to a discipline and subdue his personal appetites. The Spartan conditions and unexciting routines of monastic life that Merton endured are typical manifestations of Saturn. However, Merton was not at peace until he obtained permission to write. Only then could the Uranian energy in his chart find expression.

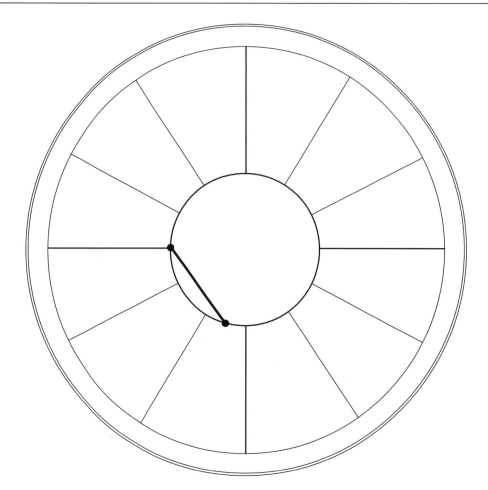

Chart 46: The Quintile—72°

The Quintile

The quintile (72°) is a challenging aspect. It has both creative and evolutionary potential for those who are willing to work through the challenges indicated through the associated planets and signs. Because it's so close to a sextile, it can look and feel like a soft aspect. However, upon closer examination, one finds that there's more challenge than compatibility in this aspect.

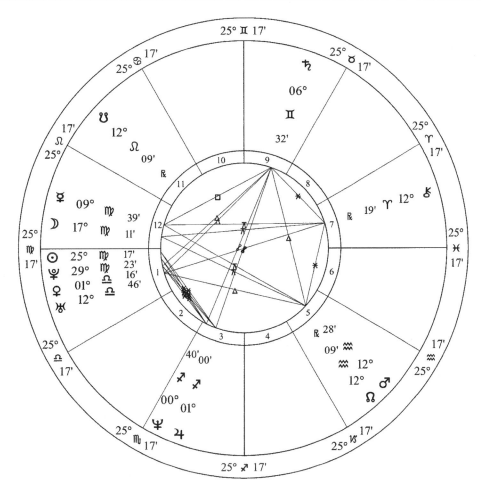

Chart 47: Lance Armstrong
September 18, 1971
Plano, Texas / Sunrise chart

Lance Armstrong: Jupiter-Neptune in Sagittarius
Quintile Mars in Aquarius and Moon in Virgo

We've seen already how Lance's Jupiter-Neptune conjunction in Sagittarius fostered a "shining belief in belief" that helped him beat cancer. It also spurred him on to the first of seven Tour de France victories. This conjunction forms two different quintiles in his chart: one with Mars in Aquarius and the other with Moon in Virgo.

In the quintile with Mars, we find two compatible elements: fire and air. Were the planets just 12° closer, this would have been a free and easy sextile, with Jupiter-Neptune fanning the flames of Mars in Aquarius and making Lance even more aggressive.

However, it was just the opposite. When Jupiter-Neptune was activated by transiting Pluto and cancer struck, it was as if someone had thrown a wrench into the machinery of Lance's seemingly unstoppable Mars: all extraneous activity came to a screeching halt. At the same time, his Moon in Virgo, forming a quintile with Jupiter-Neptune from the opposing hemisphere, came roaring to life. In the process, Lance learned how crucial the careful, analytical energy of Virgo was to the "gear-combination mathematics" of professional cycling.

In essence, the two quintiles acted as a bridge between Lance's pre-cancer and post-cancer lives. Before cancer, Mars predominated, with Lance behaving more like a combative Aries than a Virgo stellium. He rushed headlong into races, unable to heed his coach's advice and conserve energy. After cancer, Lance was able to integrate the sidelined Virgo energies into his life. Lance truly reaped the benefits of the evolutionary potential of this aspect.

Eric Harris: Sun-Mars-Venus in Aries Quintile Moon in Cancer

We've already seen the disastrous consequences of Harris's Sun-Pluto opposition: the Sun-Mars conjunction in Aries was inflamed by Pluto, a process that in turn unleashed a torrent of pent-up Plutonic rage. We're now ready to examine how a quintile between his Sun-Moon conjunction and an eighth-house Cancer Moon affected this dynamic.

There is tremendous tension in this quintile. In it, we find two incompatible elements (fire and water) and three dignified planets: Mars (ruling), Sun (exalted), and a ruling Moon in Cancer. The fact that they are all dignified imbues them with confidence bordering on hubris. By contrast, Venus in Aries, in her detriment, tends to react defensively in the presence of these headstrong planets.

In the powerful Aries conjunction we see a self-centered orientation that stops at nothing to get what it wants. Because these three planets reside in the fifth house, they need to find expression in creative, original ways. The Moon is also very personal and individualistic. But where Aries clamors after independence and autonomy, Cancer craves intimacy. That lunar desire for deep connection is deepened by the Moon's placement in the eighth house.

As we've already seen, neither the intimacy needs of his eighth-house Cancer Moon nor the Aries' urge to be number one was met. The conflict between the fire-water energies is

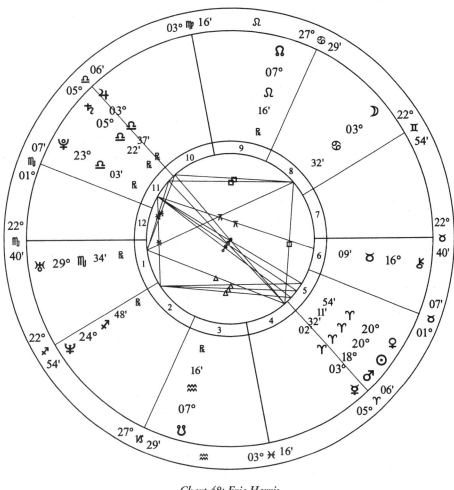

Chart 48: Eric Harris
April 9, 1981 / 9:37 p.m. CST
Wichita, Kansas / Placidus houses

heightened by the quintile aspect. Combined with the explosiveness of the Pluto opposition, these conflicts all came to a head in a rain of gunfire on April 20, 1999.

How might Harris have used this aspect to grow and evolve? With the fifth-house emphasis, creativity is tagged. We've already seen that Harris had few outlets for his creative impulses. The quintile offers yet more testimony that had Harris been given a viable outlet for these creative impulses—and a nurturing mentor figure (Moon in Cancer in the eighth) to help cultivate his talents—the Pluto energies could have been channeled in a more positive direction.

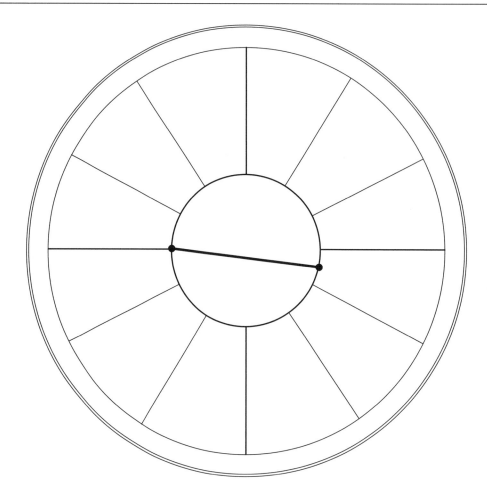

Chart 49: The Quindecile—165°

The Quindecile

Just 15° shy of an opposition, the quindecile is a hard aspect characterized by separation and upset. With this aspect, one invariably finds some sort of upheaval—sometimes physical (such as a move, a parent leaving) and sometimes emotional (such as a divorce). The trauma of separation, especially when it occurs at a formative age, creates pain, which in turn leads to an obsessive need to "put Humpty Dumpty back together again"—to rejoin the severed elements of one's life. Usually, though, this is impossible, a fact that generates yet more frustration and anger.

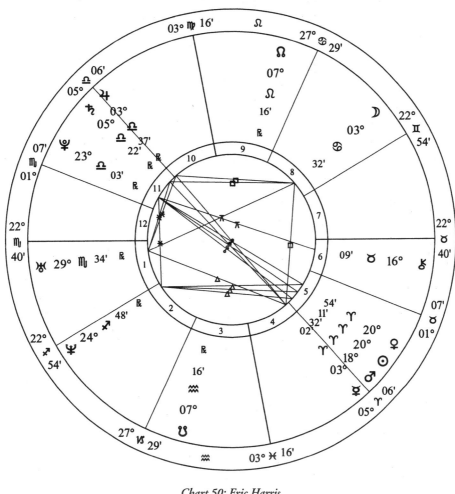

Chart 50: Eric Harris
April 9, 1981 / 9:37 p.m. CST
Wichita, Kansas / Placidus houses

Eric Harris: Mars, Sun and Venus in Aries
Quindecile Saturn and Jupiter in Libra

Let's return one final time to the chart of Eric Harris, who had several interweaving quindeciles between Mars, Sun, and Venus (18°, 20°, and 20° Aries, respectively) and Saturn and Jupiter (5° and 3° Libra).

We already know of the tremendous stress placed upon the Aries planets—not only by Pluto but by the Moon. Add to that the stress of the quindeciles, which manifested in several moves the Harris family made when Eric was still a child. Eric Harris would later say that the constant moving around left him feeling alienated and rootless.

There are two levels of separation at work here. The first is indicated by the physical moves. The second is the separation that Eric, a creative boy with three planets in the fifth house and an eighth-house Cancer Moon, felt with his military father. Indeed, the father is keyed here in several ways—through the involvement of both Saturn and Mars, and the fact that Saturn is retrograde. This left the conflicted child very isolated. It's no surprise that Eric forged such a deep bond (Moon in Cancer in the eighth) with Dylan Klebold to execute his final, desperate act.

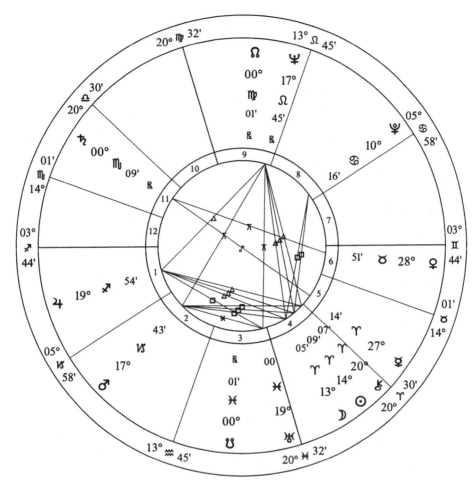

Chart 51: Marlon Brando
April 3, 1924 / 11:00 p.m. CST
Omaha, Nebraska / Placidus houses

Marlon Brando: Sun in Aries Quindecile Saturn in Scorpio

Here we see another father issue indicated through a quindecile between Sun and Saturn retrograde. Many analysts have cited the conflicts between Marlon and his father as generating much of the actor's passion on stage. The psychological upsets between father and son were aggravated by upheaval generated by moves and separations, amplifying Brando's feelings of rootlessness and insecurity.

Thomas Merton: Moon in Leo Quindecile Mercury in Aquarius

Here is a feminine symbol, the Moon, keyed to the fourth house of Merton's chart—the realm of the father/mother. (See chart on page 140.) As the quindecile would suggest, Merton's life was marked by a series of separations: his mother's death when he was six and his father's death when he was sixteen. In addition, Merton's family changed countries eight times before their son entered university and settled in the United States at age eighteen.[2]

Princess Diana: Venus in Taurus Quindecile Neptune in Scorpio

Here are two more feminine symbols, Venus and Neptune, in a quindecile. (See chart on page 138.) Interestingly, the early upset in Diana's life—her parents' divorce when she was eight—by and large involved separation from the mother, as it was Diana's father who finally gained custody.

---

1. Thomas Merton, *The Seven Storey Mountain* (New York: Harcourt Brace, 1998), p. 148.
2. Ibid.

CHAPTER TWELVE

Techniques of Transformation

Many years ago I was teaching English at a private girls' high school in Tokyo. A few students had expressed an interest in astrology, and one afternoon I invited them over and did their charts. As the first one rolled out of the printer, one of them, not knowing anything at all about astrology, squealed: "Looks bad!"

Perhaps this propensity to divide things into "good" and "bad" is a symptom of the age in which we live, or perhaps it's just human nature. In astrology, as in life, determining what is "good" or "bad," "lucky" or "unlucky," depends largely on the individual. Kurt Cobain had a chart full of trines and sextiles—the supposedly "easy" aspects—and he killed himself at age twenty-seven. Mahatma Gandhi, whose chart we will be examining shortly, had a hard aspect between Mars and Pluto—a contact often found in the charts of serial killers. Despite (or because of?) this, he was a force for good largely unparalleled in human history.

Rather than speaking of good or bad, easy or difficult, we should inquire into the nature of the challenges posed by our charts. As we've seen, hard aspects create frustration and conflicting impulses. Soft aspects, while on the surface much easier to deal with, are in some ways more dangerous because they can induce complacency and, in worst-case scenarios, grandiosity.

Ironically, hard aspects also can create a virtual complacency because of the psyche's tendency to split off unacceptable thoughts and feelings, thus creating a false sense of well-being. In both cases, astrology is a powerful tool for accessing subterranean regions of psyche and bringing them up into the light of day. The danger of leaving those aspects of self in exile is clear from our iceberg analogy: the same sunken hulk of ice that destroyed the Titanic can just as easily derail a life.

Defense Mechanisms of the Psyche

Before exploring different strategies for managing both soft and hard aspects, let's take a moment to look at some of the defense mechanisms the psyche employs to insulate the ego from the unacceptable thoughts, feelings, or memories that often accompany squares, oppositions, and conjunctions.

Repression

Repression keeps painful, shameful, or dangerous feelings and thoughts out of consciousness, including desires that run counter to the prevailing moral codes of a culture or era. We have seen how Katharine Graham repressed the deep need for intimacy and connection indicated by Venus in Cancer and Moon in Taurus because it was inappropriate in the "culture" of her overachieving family. It took her years to become aware of this process.

Splitting

Splitting is one of the ways in which infants bring order to their world by separating good from bad and differentiating the "good mother" from the "bad mother." The child is unable to bear both qualities in one human being. Although originating in infancy, splitting can and does happen throughout life as we struggle to reconcile positive and negative qualities within ourselves and others.

Projections

Another way the ego deals with unacceptable impulses is by attributing them to, or "projecting" them onto, others. Projections are often at the root of the boss we detest, the spouse we resent, or a rival co-worker. Projections are a part of everyday life and consciousness—"We cannot not project," as one psychologist friend put it. However, the more unconscious this process becomes, the more we find ourselves living in a fearful universe over which we have little control.

Techniques of Transformation: Trining Your Squares and Squaring Your Trines

As we saw in the Introduction, learning to manage the energies in your birth chart involves a delicate balance of trining your squares and squaring your trines: alchemizing the raw emotion and impulse of the hard aspects while not falling prey to the complacency inherent in soft aspects.

Let's review ways of dealing with both hard and soft aspects before considering possible diagnostic techniques.

Trining Your Squares: Strategies for Dealing with Hard Aspects

The first question we must ask when approaching hard aspects is: Am I owning each of the planetary energies? If Mars, Uranus, Pluto, or Saturn are present, chances are that there is some trauma or difficulty involved and that one or more elements are being split off or projected.

One way to begin is simply to list each of the hard-aspected planets and how they are being expressed in your life. It's important to write this down. Research indicates that the act of writing can objectify difficult memories and emotions and help us gain distance from them. Although we are only going to be looking at some very rudimentary writing activities in this chapter, let's take a moment to consider just how valuable writing can be. "The therapeutic process of writing," says writer Louise DeSalvo, "goes something like this":

> We receive a shock or a blow or experience a trauma in our lives. In exploring it, examining it, and putting it into words, we stop seeing it as a random, unexplained event. We begin to understand the order behind appearances. Expressing it in language robs the event of its power to hurt us; it also assuages our pain. And by expressing ourselves in language, by examining these shocks, we paradoxically experience delight—pleasure, even—which comes from the discoveries we make as we write.[1]

Used in conjunction with one's natal chart, we are all the more enabled to "understand the order behind appearances." Jungian analyst Robert Johnson likens the inner model of the individual (one depicted by the birth chart) to a plan for a cathedral. At first, he says, only the general contours can be seen. As years pass, "the edifice rises, stone by stone, until finally the last blocks are in place and the finishing touches are complete. Only then is the magnificent vision of the architect revealed."[2]

What a beautiful blueprint we have for this in the sacred geometry of the astrological chart, which extends out into the heavens as well as deep down into the soul. Thus, traumatic events associated with hard aspects that at first might appear devoid of meaning are in fact important elements in the master plan of the soul.

There is another reason that it's important to take time to engage, through writing or other means, each of the planets in our hard aspects: to flesh out and make explicit the inner landscape of thoughts, feelings, emotions, and impulses that, while invisible, comprise a real and vital world. For all the critiques that have been made of Freud, we have him to thank for showing us that the conscious ego is not the whole show. Indeed, the psyche is composed of an entire community of figures.

Although we know better, we often labor under the illusion that the ego is the sole voice in the psyche. How, then, can we contact this inner world and make it real? Professional musicians spend hours on rigorous ear-training exercises in order to make the invisible world of music real and alive and vital. Is the sonata in a major or minor key? Does the concerto end on the tonic or subdominant? Does the chord have four or five notes in it? So, too, do we need a means of naming and engaging with the many voices of psyche that astrologers call planets.

Cultivating Awareness: The Aspects Diagnostics Grid

The aspects diagnostics grid is a first step toward fleshing out this inner world. The chart enables us to view the function of each of the planets, as well as how the planetary energy is (or is not) being expressed in our lives. The following grid shows Katharine Graham's Venus-Pluto conjunction, how both energies were sidelined, and the alchemization that occurred with the advent of her husband's suicide.

Katharine Graham

Type of Aspect: Conjunction

Planet	Function(s)	Sign	Expression	Alchemy
♀	Intimacy, relationships	Cancer	Split off	Developed connections at work
♇	Power	Cancer	Projected	Became publisher at the *Post*

The next grid is for a private client, "Sue Ellen," a twenty-two-year-old American woman attending graduate school. When she came to see me, Sue Ellen spoke of her image of herself as a "nice girl" and a dutiful daughter, something seen through a close square between Venus and Neptune. However, Sue Ellen is also a Leo, and her Sun is in a tight square to Uranus—the signature of a rebellious leader. Many famous people with hard Sun-Uranus aspects (George Sand, Jackie Chan, and Bruce Springsteen, to name a few) are notable for breaking free of convention and blazing new trails.

When told of the Sun-Uranus contact and asked about the apparent contradiction, Sue Ellen sighed. "It's true. I watch myself in classes and I just sit there the whole time and say nothing. I can't believe I have anything important to say. Everyone else is above me. Their ideas are more creative."

Up to now, the Uranus energy has found an outlet in her life through rebellious boyfriends, ones her parents invariably have disapproved of. Here is the grid for her Sun-Uranus square:

Sue Ellen

Type of Aspect: Square

Planet	Function	Sign	Expression	Alchemy
☉	Life force	Leo	Repressed	
♅	Individuation	Libra	Projected	Rebellious boyfriends

We'll see in the next section how Sue Ellen is working to access the Leo-Uranian energies in her chart.

The following grid shows Princess Diana's Venus-Uranus square. (See also the section "The Fixed Square: Princess Diana" in chapter 2.) The chart shows how she overemphasized her need for intimacy while projecting her desire for freedom onto Charles.

Princess Diana
Type of Aspect: Square

Planet	Function(s)	Sign	Expression	Alchemy
♀	Intimacy, connection	Taurus	Overemphasized	Charitable work
♅	Freedom		Projected	

Exercise

Choose a hard aspect from your chart. Using the following grid, fill in the blanks for each planet. Feel free to create your own grid or chart, or access the planets in other ways. The important thing is to do something to concretize each of the planetary energies.

Name of Person: _____
Type of Aspect: _____

Planet	Function(s)	Sign	Expression	Alchemy
A:				
B:				

The aspects diagnostics grid represents a preliminary step in a lifelong process of becoming aware of each of the planets in our hard aspects. The "grid" is only a very crude first stab at this. We all find different ways of getting in touch with each of the planetary energies in our charts. There's no such thing as total awareness: the unconscious is so vast that there will always be something more to unearth. However, once you feel you have made a start, you're ready for the next stage.

Active Imagination

Once named and objectified, a next step is engaging each of these voices/planets in dialogue. One way of doing this is through Active Imagination, a method whereby one aspect of the psyche is personified and then engaged as though it were a separate entity. Active Imagination was developed by Carl Jung in the early twentieth century. It is one way of entering into conversation with various aspects of self that dwell in the unconscious. It is similar to dreaming, except that you are fully awake during the experience. Active Imagination is not synonymous with aimless fantasy or meandering daydreams—what medieval alchemists called the "madman's cornerstone." Rather, it is the sustained, intentional use of an imaginal idea, undertaken to forge a more unified and integrated sense of self.

For Sue Ellen, this involved tapping into her musical talent, and specifically an interest in jazz. Voicing a desire to contact the Leo/Uranian energies, Sue Ellen spoke of her love for jazz singing and how it enabled her to access ecstatic states of consciousness. However, she was extremely frustrated by not being able to express those energies in her daily life. Sadly, her singing was limited to afternoon practice sessions in her apartment—performances that no one but herself ever heard.

As a result of our discussion, Sue Ellen decided to talk to this inner singer and find out why she was so reluctant to venture out into the world. Here is the "conversation" that ensued:

Sue Ellen: Who is the singer? Why do you enter and leave my life so abruptly? Why do you not share yourself or allow yourself to be with me at school?

Helga: My name is Helga. I have been with you since the age of eight. We made a connection then that is unbreakable. It may appear at times that I have left, but it is only when you reject me. I am always with you, but you are usually unwilling to look at me. You refuse to acknowledge me out of a deep level of fear.

Sue Ellen: What is my fear?

Helga: Of not knowing where our connection will lead you. We work well on an intuitive level, and this scares you very much because your intuitive side has been rejected many times in the past.

Sue Ellen: Could you please tell me when it was rejected?

Helga: Your parents have rejected this side of you, especially your father.

Sue Ellen: Why do obstacles get in the way of my singing?

Helga: You allow them to, when you become unfocused and distracted.

Sue Ellen: Why do you not show yourself here at school?

Helga: You haven't allowed me to. You hold me back because our connection feels sacred to you, and you don't want to share me with anyone. You somewhat enjoy keeping me a secret.

Sue Ellen was visibly shaken at the end of this dialogue—a reaction that raises a very significant concern. It is best to undertake Active Imagination only when there is someone on whom we can call if the unconscious contents become overwhelming. Once this safety net has been established, there is much to be gained from the practice of Active Imagination. From Sue Ellen's brief session, we can already see that there is an unresolved conflict with her parents—one that has stunted her intuition. As a result, "Helga" has been relegated to the wings, unable to make a significant contribution to Sue Ellen's life. The resolution of this conflict will not necessarily mean that Sue Ellen will shift her career goals and become a singer, but it does suggest that she needs to find a way to bring Helga's energy and vitality into her daily life.

Exercise

Choose a planet from a hard aspect in your chart. You could select a planet that is clearly problematic, or one for which you cannot find any apparent correlations in your life (i.e., a planet that has been split off in some way). Initiate a dialogue with the planet. Be open to learning the name, gender, history, or anything else the planetary guide wants to share. Keep notes of your conversations.

Steam Control: Utilizing the Easy Places in Your Chart to Alchemize the Hard Places

Drawing on Soft Aspects, the Moon, and Jupiter

Just as Active Imagination can help us get in touch with unknown voices and untapped talents in psyche, so too can soft aspects and other low-tension areas of the birth chart provide a sort of steam control for pent-up emotions. We'll begin by looking at soft aspects.

Drawing on Soft Aspects

- Gandhi: One of the defining features of Gandhi's chart is a tough t-square between Venus-Mars in Scorpio, Jupiter-Pluto in Taurus, and a Leo Moon at the focal point. However, that Leo Moon also makes a lovely trine to Neptune in Aries. We'll see in a moment how his Moon (and the trine of which it is a part) came to the rescue more than once in his life.

- Princess Diana: We've seen how Diana's Venus-Moon-Uranus t-square wreaked havoc in her personal life, thwarting the deep intimacy needs of her Cancer Sun. However, her besieged Venus also makes a stabilizing trine to Saturn in Capricorn. On the surface, contact between Venus and Saturn might not sound very appealing. However, it is a beautiful description of how those thwarted needs for intimacy got channeled into charitable work.

Exercise

Identify a hard aspect in your chart that has expressed itself in troubling ways. Then select a trine or sextile in your chart (one that either intersects the hard aspect or is separate from it). Examine the trine by planet and sign, and explore ways that those qualities can work to offset negative tendencies of the hard aspect.

Drawing Down the Moon

The Moon is one of the paths of least resistance in the chart, a refuge from hardship and pain. (This principle, of course, must be modified when the Moon is in its detriment or fall.) It rules the fourth house, the area of the chart signifying home and psychic roots. In charts of high tension, it is one of the first places to turn for relief.

- Gandhi: Gandhi's Leo Moon indicates a flair for the theatrical. Indeed, the Mahatma's genius for theater played a big role in alchemizing the anger of his Venus-Mars-Pluto opposition. Throughout his life, Gandhi used the panache of his Leo Moon to dramatize injustice and call people to action. His Moon first made an appearance during his early years in South Africa when he galvanized the Indian community to fight discrimination by burning the hated passes that every Indian (and person of color) had to carry. His Leo Moon made a reappearance in India during the "Salt

March," when Gandhi inspired a nationwide protest against the British salt tax by leading thousands to the sea to make salt.

Using Jupiter to Ameliorate Frustration

The largest planet in the solar system, Jupiter has long been seen by astrologers as a harbinger of grace and glad tidings. Indeed, astrophysicists consider Jupiter the keystone of the solar system. Its location and gravitational power act as a protective shield that makes life on Earth possible. Jupiter also helps to deflect asteroid and comet bombardments from the solar system.

With this sort of resumé, who wouldn't look to Jupiter for help in life's travails? Even hard aspects with Jupiter rarely bring extreme difficulty. The biggest drawback to this happy planet is the danger of self-indulgence and complacency. However, when working with charts of high tension, Jupiter is one of the first places to look for relief.

- Lance Armstrong—Jupiter in Sagittarius conjunct Neptune: As we've already seen in the chapter on conjunctions (chapter 3), Lance's Jupiter played a crucial role during the early days of his battle with cancer. Later, Jupiter resurfaced after the cyclist was pronounced in remission and he was faced with the prospect of returning to his old life. But this was not an option: his old self was dead and gone. What next? After sinking into depression and playing endless rounds of golf, Lance found the courage to start his life anew after a profound spiritual awakening during a bike trip through North Carolina. Lance's "belief in belief" is the voice of Jupiter: radiant in its own sign, and suffused with the mystical power of Neptune.

- Gandhi—Jupiter in Taurus: Taurus, a fixed earth sign affiliated with the second house, denotes terra firma and concrete, this-world possessions. From his humble beginnings in South Africa where he fought discrimination to the more heady days of international acclaim, the Mahatma was devoted to the building of ashram: self-sufficient, spiritual communities that encompassed the construction of buildings, the raising of goats, and the growing of crops. John Nash also had Jupiter in Taurus. In both, we see a deep comfort in the four walls of hearth and home. With Nash in particular, home played a central role after his estranged wife agreed to let him live with her in the 1970s. This Taurean refuge, as well as the campus of Princeton University, where Nash spent many hours during his recovery, provided a "container" for his healing.

Exercise

Locate Jupiter in your chart. Describe the sign it's in. How might the characteristics of this sign work in a constructive way in your life?

The Art of Witnessing

Once you've entered into a relationship with the planets in your chart, the biggest challenge is to avoid identifying with the intense emotions that often accompany hard aspects. One way to approach this task is by developing the "witness": the still point at the center of consciousness that enables us to be present for experience. In yogic traditions, pain and difficulty—the backbend you can't master, the triangle pose that brings unbearable stress—are seen as opportunities for growth and self-discovery. The eternal challenge for the yogi is not to fight pain but to merge with it. For in fighting pain, two difficulties are created: the pain itself, and the struggle against it. When you surrender to pain, it ceases to be something hard and becomes simply what it is. "The witness does not split life into good and bad, right and wrong, high and low, or spiritual and non spiritual. It unites all of the polarities," says psychotherapist and yoga instructor Stephen Cope. "It challenges our tendency to hold on to that which we like and push away that which we don't and simply be with what is."[3]

One final word before leaving the area of hard aspects. When combinations of Uranus, Pluto, Saturn, or Mars are combined *in tandem with personal planets, particularly the Moon and Venus*, deep trauma can be signified. In such cases, the conscious ego might not be able to deal with the burden of memory that such aspects can signify. Donald Kalsched, a Jungian psychoanalyst who has worked extensively with survivors of childhood trauma, notes that not only is splitting possible, but it often becomes a *necessary* part of the process of healing.[4]

Where deep trauma has occurred, astrology can enable us to understand and unravel the underlying dynamics, but may not be sufficient to heal deep wounds. In such cases, it often helps to find a psychotherapist or analyst specialized in trauma for working through those energies.

Squaring Your Trines: Techniques for Working with Soft Aspects

Anyone who is destined to descend into a deep pit had better set about it with all the necessary precautions rather than risk falling into the hole backwards.

—Carl Jung, *Psyche and Symbol*[5]

Hard aspects can naturally lead to a working out of the planetary energies in our charts because we feel driven to do something to alleviate the pain. Not so with soft aspects, where we are often content to maintain the status quo. As a result, we must make an extra effort when dealing with these seductive places in our charts.

As with hard aspects, cultivating awareness is a good place to begin. Just as the aspects diagnostics grid can help disentangle the conflicting strains in squares and oppositions, so too can it (or other similar "diagnostics") help us navigate the eddies and currents of our soft aspects. In the process, we create a kind of inflation index: Are we avoiding the work of hard aspects by an over-reliance on our trines and sextiles? Are we becoming overly complacent? These questions, by the way, should include whether we are leaning too heavily on other easy places in our charts—dignified and exalted planets, for example. In all these cases, the same thing that in one context is a help, or even a cure, can in another context lead to disaster. Another place of refuge in the natal chart is the Moon. But here, too, lurks a danger zone. While Gandhi's Leo Moon was instrumental in defusing the tension of his volatile t-square, had he utilized it in excess it could have led to histrionics, even demagoguery. A client with Moon in Sagittarius hops on a plane and takes off for foreign climes every time there is a problem. Getting away to a totally different environment can be a huge benefit by giving us new perspectives on old problems. But used in excess, it can foster escapism.

One of the best reality checks for determining whether we're being seduced by the soft places in our charts is relationships. In the following pages we'll look at several cases where aspects between charts played a fundamental role in the individuation process.

Relationship as Spiritual Practice
Bill & Hillary: Inflation and Its Nemesis

In the chart of former president Bill Clinton, there is one square (between the Sun and Moon, with the Moon in Venus-ruled Taurus), two inconjuncts, and two double conjunctions. The rest of the chart is trines and sextiles (chart 52). It's important to note that not only do soft aspects predominate but that they are in two "soft" signs: Libra and Leo. In addition, the Sun, Moon, and Venus are all enhanced by dignity or exaltation.

Clinton's chart presents a classic study in inflation, one for which his life provides many illustrations. Sadly, Clinton the president is apt to be remembered not for his accomplishments in office but for Monicagate—his affair with White House intern Monica Lewinsky, the most notorious offspring of these inflationary energies. In addition, his famous (or rather infamous) "I didn't inhale" statement when asked whether he had ever smoked pot, and the even more absurd "It depends on what the meaning of the word 'is' is" during grand jury testimony on the Lewinsky affair, attest to Clinton's tendency to take the easy way out: a typical expression of the shadow side of soft aspects.

Clinton's equivocating behavior is especially perplexing when viewed in relation to his intellectual achievements, from his years as a Rhodes Scholar at Oxford to his graduation from Yale Law School. Intellectual precociousness is keyed astrologically by the one place in his chart where the zodiac's heavy hitters, Pluto and Saturn, make an appearance: in conjunction to Mercury. However, even his intellectual accomplishments are infected with the inflation bug. When his memoir, *My Life,* was published in 2004, the *New York Times* called it sloppy and self-indulgent. "In many ways, the book is a mirror of Mr. Clinton's presidency: lack of discipline leading to squandered opportunities; high expectations, undermined by self-indulgence and scattered concentration."[6] Here is an incisive description of the inflation that can result from an over-reliance on the "easy" places in our charts.

Psyche intervened in the form of impeachment hearings and a hostile press to offset the inflation in Clinton's chart—and in the person of Hillary Rodham. Hillary's chart provides the restraining energies so lacking in Bill's chart. Not only does her Saturn conjunct his Sun, but a Sun-Venus-Mercury conjunction in no-nonsense Scorpio in her chart squares all his Leo planets (chart 53). Interestingly, the two met when transiting Saturn was conjunct Clinton's Moon and square his Sun.

Saturn is the arch nemesis of the solar principle. Where the Sun radiates and expresses, Saturn disciplines and contracts. While antithetical, both are needed for healthy ego formation. Unbridled solar/ego energy is tantamount to looking at the Sun without protective eyewear: it is too much of an untempered good thing. Saturn is one of the forces that mediates the intensity of the solar force, in the process making it palatable for human consumption. We see Scorpio (and its ruler, Pluto) playing a similar role in the square that

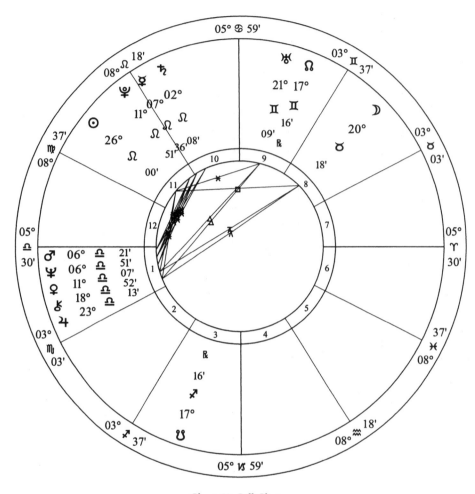

Chart 52: Bill Clinton
August 19, 1946 / 8:51 a.m. CST
Texarkana, Arkansas / Placidus houses

Hillary's Sun-Venus-Mercury conjunction makes to Bill's Leo Sun. Here is Hades, the Lord of the Underworld, making an unabashed challenge to the absolute authority of the Sun.

Being married to Hillary was not enough to save the wayward president from the scandals that nearly drove him out of office. However, one wonders where he might have ended up without her. In the final analysis, it may well come down to consciousness: through

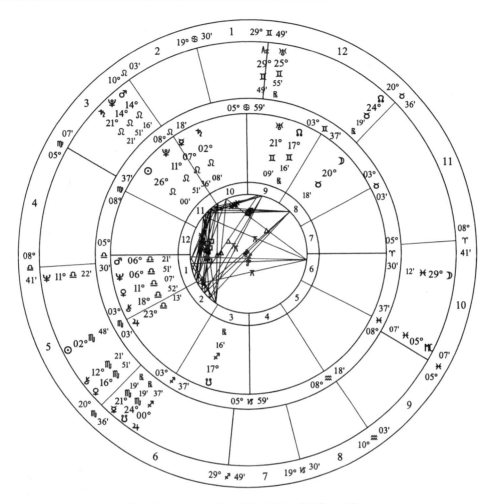

Chart 53: Synastry Biwheel for Bill and Hillary Clinton

Inner Wheel: Bill Clinton	*Outer Wheel: Hillary Clinton*
August 19, 1946 / 8:51 a.m. CST	October 26, 1947 / 8:00 p.m. CST
Texarkana, Arkansas / Placidus houses	Chicago, Illinois / Placidus houses

Hillary and other "balancing" forces, Clinton was forced to stop and reflect on his behavior—something that the sextiles and trines and exalted planets in his chart did not demand of him.

We'll now look at a very different case of Sun-Saturn in synastry.

"She Gave Him Sex, He Gave Her Class":
The Dance-Floor Magic of Ginger Rogers and Fred Astaire

This quote (courtesy of Katharine Hepburn) provides a good thumbnail sketch of the chemistry between Fred Astaire and Ginger Rogers, the legendary dance team from the 1930s. The Rogers-Astaire synastry is not only a matter of tempering inflation but of each person providing a counterweight to the other's one-sidedness.

Rogers' chart is soft and womanly: she had eight out of ten planets in yin elements (water and earth). In addition, there's a dreamy conjunction between the Sun and Neptune, as well as a Sun-Moon trine.

Astaire had eight of ten planets in fire and air, the yang elements, as well as a loose fire grand trine between Venus-Mercury, Mars, and Uranus-Saturn. Interestingly, one of his two yin planets—Sun in Taurus—sextiles Rogers' Cancer Sun. That sextile alone, however, would not have been enough for dance-floor magic. In addition, Ginger's Saturn, the unforgiving taskmaster of the zodiac, closely conjuncts Fred's Sun. How interesting that this charming and alluring woman should provide, in the form of Saturn, such a disciplining force upon Astaire's energies. One can almost see an invisible George Balanchine standing over them during rehearsals, barking out orders, keeping them in line. With Astaire's Leo Mars (the symbol of a consummate performer) sitting right on Rogers' Mercury, there was plenty of fancy footwork.

Additional Synastry Examples

Although this is not a book on synastry, a couple of other cases will help clarify just how helpful (and unhelpful) relationships can be in confronting the challenges of our charts.

First, the unhelpful case. Recall Katharine Graham's chart and particularly her Venus-Pluto conjunction in Cancer. It so happened that her husband, Phillip Graham—the one whose suicide sparked Katharine's transformation into one of the most powerful women of the twentieth century—had close conjunctions between Pluto, Mercury, Saturn, and Venus in Cancer *over the same degrees as Katharine's.* This proved to be too much for the couple to handle. As one might expect with Venus-Saturn, both husband and wife harbored feelings of massive insecurity. In the end, a process of projective identification took over whereby both projected their insecurity on the other and then vilified the other, trying desperately to push away the feelings they were so afraid of. We already know the outcome.

Now consider a very different case of a Venus-Saturn synastic overlay. Actor/director Clint Eastwood has a tight opposition between Venus in Cancer and Saturn in Capricorn. Hilary Swank, his leading lady in the 2004 blockbuster film *Million Dollar Baby,* has Venus conjunct Saturn in Cancer, which conjuncts Eastwood's Venus by three degrees. For Eastwood and Swank, this difficult overlay was one important factor in the creation of one of the best films of the decade. Of course, it helped that Swank's Leo Sun conjuncted Eastwood's Moon, and that Eastwood's Neptune tightly conjuncted Swank's Mars. It also helped that, unlike Katharine and Phil Graham, Pluto was not involved in the Venus-Saturn mix.

Putting aside, for a moment, these other mitigating factors, there is an important lesson to be learned through these synastic case studies. Unlike Katharine and Phil, Eastwood and Swank had a goal, a "third thing"—the making of a movie—through which to work out and alchemize the formidable energies symbolized by Venus and Saturn. This is also true in the case of Fred Astaire and Ginger Rogers (recall that Ginger's Saturn conjuncted Fred's Sun), who had the vessel of their choreography routines and the container of a punishing studio schedule through which to alchemize the Sun-Saturn energies.

Not true with Katharine and Phil, who had only the fragile container of their marriage. Ironically, the *Washington Post* could have provided a perfect container for the working-through of the intense energies in their charts. However, as she had done earlier in her life, Katharine sidelined herself from that process. In the final analysis, it might be that the only solution was the one that was played out: Phil's tragic suicide, and the do-or-die ultimatum that was hoisted upon Katharine as a result.

End Word

Two and a half millennia ago, a desperate man in search of enlightenment sat himself down under a Bodhi tree in Northeast India and slipped into a deep meditation. During the time he sat there, he was accosted by an array of demons who tried to terrify and ultimately destroy him. Violent storms of resentment and hatred arose. And then, worst of all, came enticing sensual delights. Through it all he remained steadfast, succumbing neither to the tempting nor the terrifying.

At the beginning of the meditation, the man's name was Prince Siddhartha. At the end, it was Shakyamuni Buddha. Indeed, the experience under the Bodhi tree proved transformative not just for one man but for all of humankind.

Think of your natal chart as a Bodhi-tree experience in miniature. All the persecutors and demons (in the form of Saturn and Pluto and Uranus) are there, as are the enticing sensual delights (Venus, Jupiter, the Moon). The demonic elements are dramatized through hard aspects, and the enticing accentuated through those flowing trines and sextiles.

Like Fred and Ginger, we need to find the "third thing" that will help us stay balanced throughout. For Rogers and Astaire, it was dance. For Hilary and Clint, it was moviemaking. For Lance Armstrong, it was cycling (and his struggle with cancer), and for Gandhi, service. Without this third thing, sitting down under the Bodhi tree can be a perilous experience. Use the gifts of your chart—both hard aspects and soft—to lead you to that third thing and, through it, to the Buddha nature that awaits at the other side of the encounter.

1. Louise DeSalvo, *Writing as a Way of Healing* (Boston: Beacon Press, 1999), p. 43.

2. Robert Johnson, *Inner Work* (New York: HarperSanFrancisco, 1986), p. 7.

3. Stephen Cope, "Standing Psychotherapy on Its Head," *Yoga Journal*, May/June 2001, pp. 172–74.

4. Donald Kalsched, *The Inner World of Trauma* (New York: Routledge, 1996), p. 37.

5. Carl Jung, *Psyche and Symbol* (Princeton, NJ: Princeton University Press, 1991), p. 70.

6. Michiko Kakutani, "A Pastiche of a Presidency: Imitating a Life," review of *My Life*, by Bill Clinton, *New York Times*, June 20, 2004.

A Primer of Basic Astrology

The Planets

For psychological purposes, the planets are placed into two categories: personal and generational. The personal planets—Sun, Moon, Mercury, Venus, and Mars—are faster moving and, as a result, indicative of individual behavior and psychology. The generational planets—Jupiter, Saturn, Uranus, Neptune, and Pluto—move more slowly and are representative of generations. All the planets can manifest as either inner drives or outer events.

The Personal Planets

- Sun: identity, life force, the father
- Moon: instincts and emotions, the feminine, the mother
- Mercury: thinking and communication
- Venus: the love impulse, the drive for connection and affiliation, esthetics
- Mars: aggression and assertion, the urge for individuation and separation

The Generational Planets

- Jupiter: expansion, faith, optimism

- Saturn: contraction, limitation, discipline, law and order

- Uranus: revolution; electricity; violent, sudden change

- Neptune: transcendence, imagination

- Pluto: survival; the unconscious; transformation; death, sex, and rebirth

The Signs

Elemental Groups

The signs are patterns of energy through which the planets operate. They are categorized according to four elemental groups: fire, air, water, and earth. The fire and air signs are "masculine" and extroverted by nature; water and earth are "feminine" and introverted.

- Fire: Aries, Leo, Sagittarius—enthusiastic, idealistic

- Air: Gemini, Libra, Aquarius—detached, cerebral, communicative

- Water: Cancer, Scorpio, Pisces—emotional, empathetic

- Earth: Taurus, Virgo, Capricorn—practical, security conscious

Element	Sign	Characteristics	Shadow Manifestations
Fire	Aries	Courageous, direct	Egotistical, foolhardy
	Leo	Dramatic, warm	Vain, domineering
	Sagittarius	Open, tolerant	Coarse, insensitive
Air	Gemini	Articulate, versatile	Superficial, restless
	Libra	Balanced, cooperative	Hedonistic, overly accommodating
	Aquarius	Humanitarian, open	Cold, aloof
Water	Cancer	Sensitive, nurturing	Self-indulgent, afraid to take risks
	Scorpio	Deep, loyal	Manipulative, secretive
	Pisces	Empathetic, spiritual	Unrealistic, self-absorbed
Earth	Taurus	Steadfast, practical	Stubborn, materialistic
	Virgo	Discriminating, unselfish	Overly critical, fault-finding
	Capricorn	Managerial, loyal	Materialistic, status-seeking

Modalities

The planets can also be categorized by three different modalities:

- Cardinal: Aries, Cancer, Libra, Capricorn—initiating, self-reliant
- Fixed: Taurus, Leo, Scorpio, Aquarius—stubborn, persistent
- Mutable: Gemini, Virgo, Sagittarius, Pisces—adaptable, impressionable

Rulerships—Dignities—Debilities

The planets and the signs are integrally connected, with each of the signs *ruled* by a planet.

Sign	Characteristics	Ruling Planet
Aries	Courageous, initiating	Mars
Taurus	Practical, dependable	Venus
Gemini	Flexible, communicative	Mercury
Cancer	Nurturing, empathetic	Moon
Leo	Warm, expressive	Sun
Virgo	Discriminating, unselfish	Mercury
Libra	Balanced, fair	Venus
Scorpio	Loyal, probing	Pluto
Sagittarius	Open, tolerant	Jupiter
Capricorn	Responsible, managerial	Saturn
Aquarius	Humanitarian, detached	Uranus
Pisces	Empathetic, compassionate	Neptune

The planets are most powerful when placed in the signs that they rule. Conversely, they are weakest when placed in the opposing signs. For example, Venus, ruler of Taurus, is in its *detriment* in Scorpio.

In addition, the planets are *exalted* in some signs and in their *fall* in others. Exalted planets are strong, but not as strong as planets in their ruling signs. Planets in their fall are also weak.[1]

Planet	Rules	Exaltation	Detriment	Fall
Sun	Leo	Aries	Aquarius	Libra
Moon	Cancer	Taurus	Capricorn	Scorpio
Mercury	Gemini	Virgo	Pisces	Leo
Venus	Taurus, Libra	Pisces	Aries	Virgo
Mars	Aries	Capricorn	Taurus	Cancer
Jupiter	Sagittarius	———	Gemini	———
Saturn	Capricorn	Libra	Cancer	Aries
Uranus	Aquarius	Scorpio	Leo	Taurus
Neptune	Pisces	Cancer	Virgo	Capricorn
Pluto	Scorpio	———	———	———

Aspects

Aspects are angular relationships between the planets, measured in degrees. It is useful to think of the zodiac as a 360° pie, which, when sliced, produces these angular relationships. Cutting the pie into two large pieces and placing planets at either end produces an *opposition.* Cutting it into three pieces produces *trines.* When divided into four pieces *squares* are produced; and into six, *sextiles.*

Aspects reveal the intensity of life experience, as well as how the planetary energies relate to each other. Aspects can be likened to a kind of chemical reaction in which the vibrations of the planets combine and form a third energetic entity.[2] Depending on the strength and position of the planets, the aspects can create very powerful impulses within the psyche.

There are two kinds of aspects: hard and soft (or difficult and easy).

The hard aspects bring challenge and conflict to the individual. They combine incompatible or opposing elements and require that the native employ both creativity and forbearance in order to make them work constructively. For example, say Mars in Aries (fire) squares Moon in Cancer (water) in a chart. Fire and water do not ordinarily get along, so the native must find a way of making this combination work. One solution—putting water in a pot and the pot on a hot stove—indicates just how productive these difficult aspects can be.

The hard aspects are:

- The square—90°
- The opposition—180°
- The conjunction—0°

Easy aspects combine the same or similar elements. Mars at 23° Virgo (earth) aspecting Saturn at 23° Scorpio (water) sextiles that planet. The Sun at the first degree of Aries (fire) aspecting Venus at the first degree of Leo (fire) is said to trine that planet. Both are examples of harmonious interactions. Soft aspects create pleasure and easy, but usually unremarkable, creativity.

The soft aspects are:

- The sextile—60°
- The trine—120°

Orbs indicate the arc within which an aspect exerts influence. Most astrologers accept an orb of 7°, sometimes larger for the Sun and Moon.

The Houses

The houses are fields of life experience. They are:

- First house: physical body, persona
- Second house: personal values and possessions
- Third house: communication, short trips
- Fourth house: home, feelings, psychic roots, the mother
- Fifth house: creativity, children
- Sixth house: physical health, service, routine working environment
- Seventh house: marriage, one-to-one relationships, opponents

- Eighth house: transformation, death, sexuality, other people's resources
- Ninth house: metaphysics, long trips
- Tenth house: career, life path, the father
- Eleventh house: friends, community, aspirations
- Twelfth house: mysticism, the unconscious, confinement

1. Traditional rulerships, dignities, exaltations, and detriments are sometimes different from those of modern astrology.
2. Alan Oken, *Alan Oken's Complete Astrology* (New York: Bantam Books, 1988), p. 386.

Chart Sources

The Rodden rating system was used for the charts in this book.*

1. Mahatma Gandhi—October 2, 1869, Porbandar, India, 7:11 a.m. LMT. Rating: C.

2. Lance Armstrong—September 18, 1971, Plano, Texas. Not rated. Sunrise chart used.

3. Eric Harris—April 9, 1981, Wichita, Kansas, 9:37 p.m. CST. Rating: AA.

4. Princess Diana—July 1, 1961, Sandringham, England, 7:45 p.m. GMD. Rating: A.

5. Princess Masako—December 9, 1963, Tokyo, Japan. Not rated. Sunrise chart used.

6. Katharine Graham—June 16, 1917, New York, New York. Not rated. Graham was born at home and no time was listed on her birth certificate. Birth time adjusted to 8:43 a.m. EST by author.

7. Charles Schulz—November 26, 1922, St. Paul, Minnesota. Not rated. Birth time adjusted to 7:07 p.m. CST by author.

8. Martha Stewart—August 3, 1941, Jersey City, New Jersey, 1:33 p.m. EDT. Rating: AA.

9. Rush Limbaugh—January 12, 1951, Cape Girardeau, Missouri, 7:50 a.m. CST. Rating: AA.

10. Jane Fonda—December 21, 1937, Manhattan, New York, 9:14 a.m. EST. Rating: AA.

11. Kurt Cobain—February 20, 1967, Aberdeen, Washington, 7:20 p.m. PST. Rating: AA.

12. Katharine Hepburn—May 12, 1907, Hartford, Connecticut, 5:47 p.m. EST. Rating: AA.

13. John Nash—June 13, 1928, Bluefield, West Virginia, 7:00 a.m. EST. Rating: AA.

14. Marlon Brando—April 3, 1924, Omaha, Nebraska, 11:00 p.m. CST. Rating: AA.

15. Muhammad Ali—January 17, 1942, Louisville, Kentucky, 6:35 p.m. CST. Rating: AA.

16. United States of America—July 4, 1776, Philadelphia, Pennsylvania, 3:10 a.m. LMT. Not rated.

17. Henry Miller—December 26, 1891, Manhattan, New York, 12:30 p.m. EST. Rating: A.

18. Thomas Merton—January 31, 1915, Prads, France, 9:00 a.m. GMT. Rating: AA.

19. Bill Clinton—August 19, 1946, Texarkana, Arkansas, 8:51 a.m. CST. Rating: A.

20. Hillary Clinton—October 26, 1947, Chicago, Illinois, 8:00 p.m. CST. Rating: DD.

* *Rodden Rating System:*

AA   Accurate data as recorded by the family or state.

A   Accurate data as quoted by the person, kin, friend, or associate.

B   Biography or autobiography.

C   Caution: no source.

DD   Dirty data—two or more conflicting quotes that are unqualified.

X   Data with no time of birth.

XX   Data without a known or confirmed date.

From: http://www.astrodatabank.com.

Bibliography

Andersen, Hans Christian. *The Red Shoes.* 1845. Reprint, La Jolla, CA: Green Tiger Press, 1982.

Armstrong, Lance, with Sally Jenkins. *It's Not About the Bike.* New York: Berkley Books, 2000.

Barton, Tamsyn. *Ancient Astrology.* New York: Routledge, 1994.

A Beautiful Mind. Film directed by Ron Howard. Universal Video, 2002.

Berger, M. "Katharine Graham of Washington Post Dies at 84." *New York Times*, July 18, 2001, p. 1.

Berzoff, Joan, Laura Melano Flanagan, and Patricia Hertz. *Inside Out and Outside In.* Northvale, NJ: Jason Aronson, 1996.

Bosworth, Patricia. *Marlon Brando.* New York: Viking, 2001.

Brandon, J. "Americans Must Correct Their Ignorance of Asia." Op-ed page, *International Herald Tribune*, October 23, 2001.

Burdick Harmon, Melissa. "The Transformation of Katharine Graham," *Biography*, March 2003.

Campion, Nick. "Liz Greene Interview Part 2: The Lens of Astrology." *Mountain Astrologer* (February-March, 2002): p. 39.

Carlson, M., and J. M. Horowitz. "The Accidental Feminist." *Time*, February 17, 1997, p. 24.

Chadha, Yogesh. *Gandhi: A Life.* New York: John Wiley, 1997.

Childs, K. "Kay Graham's Side of the Story." *Editor & Publisher*, November 15, 1997, p. 17.

Chin, P. "Gentle Genius." *People*, February 28, 2000, pp. 54–59.

Cope, Stephen. "Standing Psychotherapy on Its Head." *Yoga Journal,* May/June 2001, pp. 172–74.

Cummins, C. "Life Without Sex?" *Yoga Journal,* November 2002, p. 96.

Cunningham, Donna. *Astrology and Spiritual Development.* San Rafael, CA.: Cassandra Press, 1989.

DeSalvo, Louise. *Writing as a Way of Healing.* Boston: Beacon Press, 1999.

Diagnostic and Statistical Manual of Mental Disorders, IV. Washington D.C.: American Psychiatric Association, 2000.

Edgerton, C. "Katharine Graham." *Entertainment Weekly*, January 4, 2002, p. 37.

Edinger, Edward. *Ego and Archetype.* Boston: Shambhala, 1992.

Erlanger, S. "In Europe, Some Scold 'World's Policeman.'" Op-ed page, *New York Times*, September 26, 2001.

Faiola, A. "Princess Masako Bears Royal Burden." *Washington Post*, June 25, 2004, p. 1.

Felsenthal, Carol. *Power, Privilege, and the Post: The Katharine Graham Story.* New York: Seven Stories Press, 1993.

Fortune, Dion. *The Training and Work of an Initiate.* York Beach, ME: Samuel Weiser, 2000.

Fritchey, P. "She Moved to an Inner Life." *Newsweek*, July 30, 2001, p. 57.

Gandhi. Film directed by Richard Attenborough. Columbia Video, 1982.

Gandhi, M. K. *An Autobiography.* Ahmedabad, India: Navajivan Trust, 1927.

Gauquelin, Michel. *Cosmic Influences on Human Behavior.* Santa Fe, NM: Aurora Press, 1994.

Gibbs, N., and T. Roche. "The Columbine Tapes." *Time*, December 20, 1999, p. 46.

Giles, J. "The Poet of Alienation." *Newsweek*, April 18, 1994, pp. 33–38.

Goode, E. "Wanted: Brave and Congenial." *International Herald Tribune*, February 12, 2003.

Graham, Katharine. *Personal History.* New York: Vintage Books, 1998.

Halberstam, David. *The Powers That Be.* New York: Dell, 1979.

Hamaker-Zondag, Karen. *The Yod Book.* York Beach, ME: Samuel Weiser, 2000.

Hays, C., and D. Carr. "Before Facing Judge, Stewart Is Out and About." Business section, *New York Times*, July 15, 2004, p. 1.

Hepburn, Katharine, host. *All About Me.* Video directed by David Heeley. Turner Pictures, 1992.

Hillman, James. *Re-Visioning Psychology.* New York: HarperPerennial, 1975.

The Holy Bible. The Old Testament, revised standard edition. San Francisco: Ignatius Press, 1952.

Johnson, Robert. *Inner Work.* New York: HarperSanFrancisco, 1986.

Jung, Carl. *Psyche and Symbol.* Princeton, NJ: Princeton University Press, 1991.

Kakutani, Michiko. "A Pastiche of a Presidency: Imitating a Life." Review of *My Life*, by Bill Clinton. *New York Times*, June 20, 2004.

Kalsched, Donald. *The Inner World of Trauma.* New York: Routledge, 1996.

Koh, T. "The Ignorance on Both Sides Can Cause Trouble." *International Herald Tribune*, July 26, 2001, p. 4.

Krishnamurti, J. *Freedom from the Known.* Hampshire, UK: Krishnamurti Foundation Trust Ltd., 1969.

Lhalungpa, Lobsang P., trans. *The Life of Milarepa.* New York: Penguin Books, 1977.

Lyman, R. "Marlon Brando, Oscar-Winning Actor, Is Dead at 80." *New York Times*, July 2, 2004, p. 1.

Martin, Claire. "Cycling Becomes Metaphor for Cancer Battle." *Denver Post*, June 4, 2000.

Martin, Jay. *Always Merry and Bright: The Life of Henry Miller.* New York: Penguin, 1978.

Meachum, Virginia. *Martha Stewart: Successful Businesswoman.* Berkeley Heights, NJ: Enslow Publishers, 1998.

Merton, Thomas. *The Seven Storey Mountain.* New York: Harcourt Brace, 1998.

Moses, L. "U.S. Newspapers' Leading Lady." *Editor & Publisher*, July 23, 2001, p. 10.

Nasar, Sylvia. *A Beautiful Mind.* New York: Touchstone, 1998.

Oken, Alan. *Alan Oken's Complete Astrology.* New York: Bantam Books, 1988.

Onishi, N. "A Princess's Distress Pierces Japan's Veil of Secrecy." *New York Times*, August 7, 2004.

Reagan, N. "With Great Friendships, You Don't Try to Figure Them Out." *Newsweek,* July 30, 2001, p. 58.

Reich, Wilhelm. *Character Analysis.* New York: Touchstone, 1945.

Remnick, David. *King of the World: Muhammad Ali and the Rise of an American Hero.* New York: Random House, 1998.

Rosenblatt, R. "Why So Many New Yorkers Are Crazy About the Place." *International Herald Tribune,* November, 23, 2001.

Rudhyar, Dane. *Person-Centered Astrology.* New York: Aurora Press, 1980.

Schlesinger, A., Jr. "In Vindicating Herself She Became a Quiet Revolutionary." *Newsweek*, July 30, 2001, p. 55.

———. Review of *Power, Privilege, and the Post: The Katharine Graham Story*, by Carol Felsenthal. *New Republic*, May 3, 1993, p. 36.

Sciolino, E. "Who Hates Us? Who Loves Us?" Op-ed page, *New York Times*, September 23, 2001.

Siegel, Bernie. *Love, Medicine & Miracles.* New York: HarperCollins, 1986.

Thomas, E. "An American Original." *Newsweek*, July 30, 2001, p 48.

Tyl, Noel. *The Creative Astrologer.* St. Paul, MN: Llewellyn Publications, 2000.

———. *Synthesis & Counseling in Astrology.* St. Paul, MN: Llewellyn Publications, 1994.

Wilford, J. N. "Solar System's 'Cousin' Found." *New York Times*, June 14, 2002, p. A1.

Wolf, Ernest. *Treating the Self.* New York: Guilford Press, 1988.

Yogananda, Paramahansa. *Autobiography of a Yogi.* Los Angeles: Self-Realization Fellowship, 2001.